MAKERS
of the
MUSLIM
WORLD

Ibn Taymiyya

JON HOOVER

ONEWORLD
ACADEMIC

Oneworld Academic
An imprint of Oneworld Publications Ltd

Published by Oneworld Academic, 2019
Reprinted, 2021, 2025

A CIP record for this title is available from the British Library

ISBN 978-1-78607-689-2
eISBN 978-1-78607-690-8

Map © Erica Milwain

Typeset by Geethik Technologies
Printed and bound in Great Britain by Clays Ltd, Elcograf S.p.A.

The authorised representative in the EEA is eucomply OÜ, Pärnu mnt 139b–14, 11317 Tallinn, Estonia
(email: hello@eucompliancepartner.com / phone: +33757690241)

Oneworld Publications Ltd
10 Bloomsbury Street
London WC1B 3SR
England

MAKERS
of the
MUSLIM
WORLD

Ibn Taymiyya

TITLES IN THE MAKERS OF THE MUSLIM WORLD SERIES

Series Editors: Professor Khaled El-Rouayheb, Harvard University, and Professor Sabine Schmidtke, Institute for Advanced Study, Princeton

'Abd al-Ghani al-Nabulusi, Samer Akkach
'Abd al-Malik, Chase F. Robinson
Abd al-Rahman al-Kawakibi, Itzchak Weismann
'Abd al-Rahman III, Maribel Fierro
'Abd al-Rahman b. 'Amr al-Awza'i, Steven C. Judd
Abu Nuwas, Philip F. Kennedy
Ahmad al-Mansur, Mercedes García-Arenal
Ahmad ibn Hanbal, Christopher Melchert
Ahmad Riza Khan Barelwi, Usha Sanyal
Aisha al-Ba'uniyya, Th. Emil Homerin
Akbar, André Wink
Al Ma'mun, Michael Cooperson
Al-Mutanabbi, Margaret Larkin
Amir Khusraw, Sunil Sharma
Ashraf 'Ali Thanawi, Muhammad Qasim Zaman
Beshir Agha, Jane Hathaway
Chinggis Khan, Michal Biran
Elijah Muhammad, Herbert Berg
Fazlallah Astarabadi and the Hurufis, Shahzad Bashir
Ghazali, Eric Ormsby
Hasan al-Banna, Gudrun Krämer
Husain Ahmad Madani, Barbara D. Metcalf
Ibn 'Abd al-Wahhab, Michael Crawford
Ibn 'Arabi, William C. Chittick
Ibn Tufayl, Taneli Kukkonen
Ikhwan al-Safa', Godefroid de Callataÿ
Imam Shafi'i, Kecia Ali
Karim Khan Zand, John R. Perry
Mehmed Ali, Khaled Fahmy
Mu'awiya ibn Abi Sufyan, R. Stephen Humphreys
Muhammad Abduh, Mark Sedgwick
Mulla Sadra, Sayeh Meisami
Nasser, Joel Gordon
Nazira Zeineddine, Miriam Cooke
Sa'di, Homa Katouzian
Shah 'Abbas, Sholeh A. Quinn
Shaykh Mufid, Tamima Bayhom-Daou
Usama ibn Munqidh, Paul M. Cobb

For current information and details of other books in the series, please visit oneworld-publications.com/makers-of-the-muslim-world

For Mark and Yasmin

CONTENTS

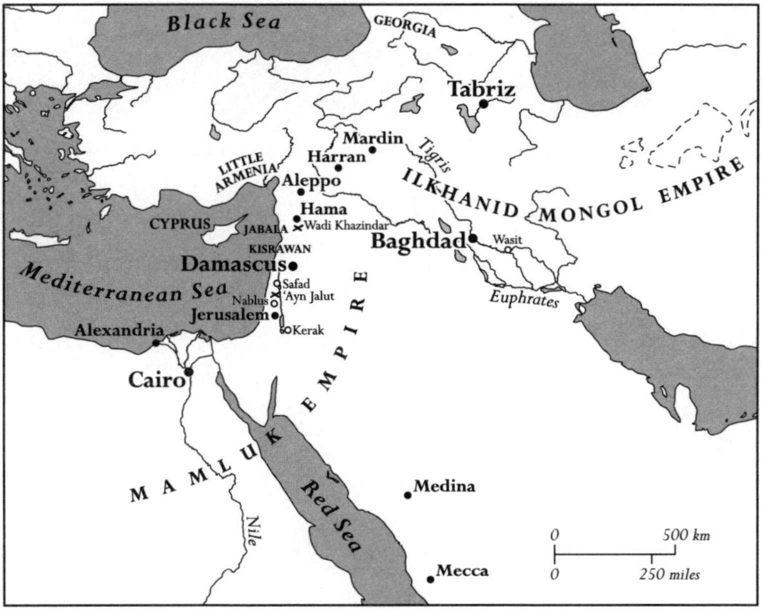

The Middle East in the late thirteenth and early fourteenth centuries

INTRODUCTION

Ibn Taymiyya of Damascus was a famous Sunni Muslim activist, jurist, and theologian. He is well-known as one of the most learned and controversial religious scholars of medieval Islam. He promoted jihad against the Mongol invaders of Syria in the early 1300s, and he challenged the dominant religious beliefs and practices of his day. Ibn Taymiyya believed that weakness in the religious life of the Mamluk Empire of Egypt and Syria had made Muslims vulnerable to invasion by the Mongol hordes from the east. Both the Mongols on the outside and religious decay on the inside had to be fought. The Mamluk elites gladly made use of Ibn Taymiyya's services to the Empire against the Mongols, but they were not always happy to tolerate his interventions in religious affairs. He endured a number of trials and imprisonments and eventually died in a Damascus prison in 1328.

Today, Ibn Taymiyya is both influential and fiercely contested. Advocates of violent jihad from the late 1970s to the present quote Ibn Taymiyya more than any other medieval scholar. Muslim modernists and contemporary revivalists reject the jihadi reading of Ibn Taymiyya and draw on his writings to address the challenges of modernity and globalization. The Arabian Wahhabi and Global Salafism movements look to Ibn Taymiyya to provide the broad outlines of their theology and spirituality. Shi'is and many Sunnis blame Ibn Taymiyya for introducing excessive intolerance and theological error into their religion. A few governments have even tried to ban his books.

Ibn Taymiyya is not always what his modern admirers and detractors make him out to be. This book aims to provide a more accurate picture of Ibn Taymiyya through a historical account of his life and thought based on recent research. The first two chapters narrate the events of Ibn Taymiyya's life. They also date his major works and discuss several shorter writings, especially those in conjunction with the Mongol invasions. The subsequent six chapters examine Ibn

Taymiyya's thought thematically. Chapters Three and Four focus on his spirituality and his polemic against innovation in religious ritual. The end of Chapter Four considers his relationship to the Islamic spirituality of Sufism. Chapter Five investigates his methodology for deriving the divine law. Chapter Six expounds Ibn Taymiyya's social and political ethics, and the end of the chapter discusses his view of jihad. Chapters Seven and Eight treat his theology. I pause intermittently throughout the book to note how later generations have used and interpreted Ibn Taymiyya's ideas, and I also consider the reception of his thought in a brief epilogue.

Several themes recur in Ibn Taymiyya's life and writings. These include his struggle against innovation in religious practice and theology, his reform-minded appeal to the foundational sources of Islam, his Sunni sectarianism over against Shi'ism and Christianity, and his apologetic conviction that Islamic revelation corresponds to reason. I have sought especially to bring out the utilitarianism that pervades Ibn Taymiyya's actions, ethics, and theology. Overarching all of these themes, however, is his practical concern that God alone be worshipped and that God be worshipped according to the divine law. Worship as obedience lies at the core of Ibn Taymiyya's mission. Ibn Taymiyya is historically significant because with intellectual power he injected a highly ethicized vision of worship into medieval Islam. His vision had only modest impact in his own time, but it has borne much fruit in later centuries, especially in modernity.

This is the first book-length academic introduction to Ibn Taymiyya in English. The pace of research on Ibn Taymiyya has quickened over the last few decades, and the time is ripe for a synthesis. The main studies used in the writing of this book are listed in the second part of the bibliography. I also had frequent recourse to the Arabic sources to fill in gaps in the research and clarify ambiguities. References for direct quotations and collections of Ibn Taymiyya's works are given in abbreviated form in the text. The key to the abbreviations is to be found in the first section of the bibliography.

I would like to thank Khaled El-Rouayheb for inviting me to write this book and the British Academy for the mid-career fellowship that provided the time to do it. I also extend my deepest gratitude to Emrah Kaya, Jabir Sani-Maihula, Seerwan Ahmed, and Zeynep Yucedogru for their insights on Ibn Taymiyya; to Ali-reza Bhojani, Azhar Majothi, Bill Janzen, Caterina Bori, Hugh Goddard, Jacqueline Hoover, Janice Hoover, Livnat Holtzman, Mohammed Al Dhfar, Mustafa Monjur, Penny Wallace, Yossef Rapoport, and anonymous readers, for commenting on draft material and helping to improve the accuracy and accessibility of the text; and to the editorial team at Oneworld Publications for their expert and professional assistance. Errors that remain are my own.

1

EARLY CAREER AND THE MONGOL INVASIONS

In 1258 the Mongol general Hulagu conquered Baghdad, the long-standing seat of the Sunni caliphate, and extended the Ilkhanid Mongol Empire throughout the traditional Sunni heartlands of Persia and Iraq. Hulagu was probably a shamanist. His wife was a Christian. The Mongol policy of treating religious communities even-handedly demoted Sunnis from their position of dominance and improved the lot of Christians and Shi'is. The Mongols also pushed west into Syria and Anatolia, and it fell to the Mamluk Empire of Egypt and Syria to halt their advance. In 1260 the Mamluks turned the Mongols back at the battle of 'Ayn Jalut in Palestine. Nonetheless, the Mongols continued to threaten the Mamluks for decades to come. It was into this world of Mongol ascendancy that Ibn Taymiyya was born.

THE FORMATIVE YEARS

Ahmad Ibn Taymiyya was born in Harran on January 22, 1263 (Rabi' al-awwal 10, 661 in the Islamic calendar). The family name "Ibn Taymiyya" means "Son of Taymiyya" in Arabic. "Taymiyya" is a woman's name. Ibn Taymiyya's disciple and primary biographer Ibn 'Abd al-Hadi offers two different explanations for the name. One is that an ancestor named his daughter Taymiyya after returning from travel in the Tayma' region of northwestern Arabia. The other is that an ancestor's mother was a preacher named Taymiyya. Harran is today in southeastern Turkey, just north of the border with Syria. At the time of Ibn Taymiyya's birth, the city was under the control of the Mamluk Empire, but that did not last for long. The Ilkhanid Mongols were close at hand. In 1269, when Ibn Taymiyya was six years old, a Mongol incursion forced his family to flee Harran for Damascus. According to Ibn 'Abd al-Hadi, the family escaped by night with their books in a cart.

Ibn Taymiyya came from a family of religious scholars affiliated with the Hanbali law school. The Hanbalis were the smallest of the four Sunni law schools within the Mamluk Empire. The Shafi'is were the largest, followed by the Hanafis and the Malikis. Religious learning was the chief route to prestige and social power in Damascus apart from the military, and Ibn Taymiyya's family was well prepared to compete in this environment. Once in Damascus, the family took up residence in the Sukkariyya madrasa, a Hanbali religious school, and Ibn Taymiyya's father became the headmaster.

Ibn Taymiyya was educated in the religious sciences, with the majority of his teachers Hanbalis. He was a precocious student well-known for his intelligence and superb memory, and he is said to have started issuing legal opinions (fatwas) by the age of 19. When his father died in 1284, Ibn Taymiyya took over the headship of the Sukkariyya madrasa, and he taught his inaugural lesson in the presence of several leading scholars. A month later, he began teaching Qur'an interpretation on Fridays at the great Umayyad mosque in the center of Damascus. Ibn Taymiyya's fame spread widely and he rose in public stature. In 1296 he attained a teaching post at the prestigious Hanbaliyya madrasa in Damascus.

APPEARANCE, CHARACTER, AND PERSONAL RELATIONSHIPS

The mature Ibn Taymiyya was a formidable figure. His prominent contemporary and erstwhile colleague Shams al-Din al-Dhahabi depicts him as follows:

> He is loved by scholars and persons of piety, soldiers and emirs, merchants and people in authority. The rest of the common people love

> him because he stands up for their benefit, day and night, in his words and his writings. As for his courage, proverbial tales are told of it, and in some of them he resembles the greatest heroes… Vehemence possessed him when he worked as if he were a fighting lion… He was frequently tactless and argumentative, may God forgive him. He was poor, having no money, and his clothing – like any other jurist – was a wide robe, a long coat, a turban worth thirty dirhams, and cheap shoes. He had short hair. His figure was daunting. His gray hair was sparse. His beard was round. His complexion was between fair and the color of grain. He was of medium height, and it was as if his eyes were two eloquent tongues above his shoulders. He led people in the longest of prayers, bowing and prostrating. Sometimes he would get up to greet a person who had arrived from a journey, and sometimes he would turn away from him. When he arrived somewhere people sometimes rose to greet him, but for him it was all the same because he was unconcerned with formalities. He never bowed to anybody, restricting himself to greeting, shaking hands and smiling. He might honor his companion on one occasion and then offend him repeatedly in dispute on other occasions. (*Nubdha* 334–335, translation adapted from 343–344)

Al-Dhahabi presents a mixed picture. On the one hand, Ibn Taymiyya is popular, courageous, devoted to religious practice, and modest in attire. Laudatory biographers such as Ibn ʻAbd al-Hadi underline the valiant and devout side of Ibn Taymiyya, and they portray him as faithful to a Hanbali ideal of moderate asceticism and piety. He did not clothe himself in rags like extreme Sufis who wished to accentuate their poverty, nor did he wear luxurious clothes that would draw attention to himself. He was generous and little concerned for food or money. He was dedicated to performing his prayers and supplications to God. On the other hand, al-Dhahabi describes Ibn Taymiyya as sometimes irritable, contentious, and rude. Other contemporary biographers depict these aspects of Ibn Taymiyya's character in a heroic light or gloss over them.

Ibn Taymiyya never married. Islamic law and the Hanbali ascetic ideal prescribe marriage, but the biographers neither criticize nor explain this lapse in Ibn Taymiyya's devotion. Celibacy was not unheard of in medieval Islam, and Ibn Taymiyya may have sacrificed marriage for the benefit of his scholarly vocation. Still, Ibn Taymiyya did not go without human companionship. He was close to his mother and his brothers Sharaf al-Din and Zayn al-Din. His brothers were also part of his intimate circle of students and fellow scholars. This group was never very large – perhaps ten or so in number – and its membership fluctuated. Al-Dhahabi had been part of the circle until losing patience with Ibn Taymiyya's embarrassing behavior and eccentric views. The Sufi 'Imad al-Din al-Wasiti functioned as a spiritual guide within the group until his death in 1311. Ibn Qayyim al-Jawziyya, Ibn Taymiyya's foremost disciple, joined the circle from 1313 onward. By and large, members of the circle shared Ibn Taymiyya's intellectual outlook and joined in with his public activism against vice and religious innovations.

EARLY ENGAGEMENTS WITH RELIGIOUS LAW

Ibn Taymiyya devoted much energy in his late twenties and early thirties to religious law. His treatise on the rites of pilgrimage (MF 26:98–159) likely dates to 1292 when, at the age of 29, he performed the pilgrimage to Mecca. This treatise expresses imperatives that will dominate his thinking throughout his career: perform the prescribed religious rituals according to the pattern of the earliest Muslim generations (known as the Salaf), avoid innovated and unauthorized practices (*bid'a*), and worship God alone.

Ibn Taymiyya's *Commentary on The Support* (*Sharh al-'umda*) probably dates to the mid-1290s, and it illustrates Ibn Taymiyya's early conformity to Hanbali law. This bulky work annotates the sections on religious ritual in *The Support* (*al-'Umda*), a survey of mainstream Hanbali legal positions by the eminent scholar Muwaffaq al-Din Ibn Qudama (d. 1223). Throughout the *Commentary*, Ibn Taymiyya faithfully conforms to the rulings of the Hanbali school, as was expected of jurists in their respective law schools at the time.

In his later years, however, Ibn Taymiyya sometimes departs from Hanbali views. Al-Dhahabi writes, "For some years now he has not issued legal opinions according to a specific school, but rather according to the proof that supports his position" (*Nubdha* 333). To take one example, Ibn Taymiyya in his *Commentary* follows the Hanbalis in making the lesser pilgrimage to Mecca (*'umra*) obligatory. Later on, he states that it is optional, a view that happens to agree with the Malikis and the Hanafis (MF 26:5–9). Ibn Taymiyya argues this case directly from the Qur'an. He does not take the Hanbali view, nor the view of any other school, to be binding. Ibn Taymiyya is here exercising what is called "independent reasoning" (*ijtihad*), a practice that broke with the protocol of the Sunni law school system of his day. We will encounter further implications of Ibn Taymiyya's independent reasoning at different points in this book, and especially in Chapter Five.

A third early work on law dicusses punishment for insulting the Prophet Muhammad. The occasion of this treatise was Ibn Taymiyya's first major intervention in public affairs. The story begins in mid-1294 when he was 31 years old. People from a village just outside Damascus complained directly to the governor of the city that a Christian scribe had insulted the Prophet. Insulting the Prophet was a capital offense. The governor ignored the complaint out of deference to the Christian's employer, an emir named 'Assaf. This displeased Ibn Taymiyya and the Shafi'i jurist Zayn al-Din al-Fariqi. They led a crowd from the Umayyad mosque in the center of Damascus to visit the governor. The governor assured them that the Christian would be treated according to the religious law. At the same time, a crowd pelted the emir 'Assaf with stones at one of the city gates. 'Assaf escaped. The governor learned of the uproar and had Ibn Taymiyya and other agitators beaten and confined.

Then the governor looked for a way out of his legal predicament. The next day he sent representatives to the village. They tried to invalidate the complaint by showing that some prior enmity had divided the complainants and the Christian. This failed. The Christian then converted to Islam in a bid to avoid death. Conversion annulled the death penalty in mainstream Shafi'i legal doctrine. A week later, the governor summoned the Shafi'i chief judge of Damascus and other Shafi'i jurists. He asked whether the Christian's conversion to Islam could spare his life. All of the Shafi'is said yes. The governor almost certainly knew that Shafi'i legal doctrine would give him the judgement he desired. The agitator al-Fariqi was questioned as well, and he concurred with his Shafiʻi colleagues. Ibn Taymiyya was released without being asked about his view – the governor probably knew that he would differ.

The following week the governor called the chief judges of the four Sunni legal schools together to discuss the case. It was Mamluk practice that a chief judge from each of the four schools sat on the governor's court. The governor was probably trying to get all of them to recognize the Shafiʻi ruling so that the Christian convert to Islam could be freed. According to the protocols of the day, the non-Shafiʻis did not need to agree with the Shafiʻis. They only needed to concede the governor's prerogative to choose the judgement of the law school that best suited his purposes. This time, however, no agreement was reached. The Hanafi chief judge wrote a poem claiming that the law schools had in fact come to consensus on the opposite view: someone who insults the Prophet cannot escape the death penalty by converting to Islam. The religious law was not flexible enough to give the governor what he wanted. Nonetheless, he still found a way to achieve his ends: about four months later, the convert was released under the cover of night.

Writing not as a judge but as a legal scholar, Ibn Taymiyya composed his book *The Sword Unsheathed* (*al-Sarim al-maslul*) to affirm that repentance and conversion do not avert the death penalty for insulting the Prophet. This work is the most comprehensive discussion of the topic in the Islamic tradition. Ibn Taymiyya's intervention in the case of the Christian scribe who insulted the Prophet established his reputation as a force to be reckoned with on the Damascene scholarly and political scene.

EARLY ENGAGEMENTS WITH THEOLOGY

The 1290s also saw the beginnings of the theological controversies that would eventually land Ibn Taymiyya in a Cairo prison in 1306. In 1291 opponents tried to stop him from teaching in the Umayyad mosque on Fridays because of some comments he had made on God's attributes. The affair ended quickly when the Shafiʿi chief judge and another scholar defended him.

Seven years later, Ibn Taymiyya wrote two short theological pieces that drew much attention in his own time and are today core doctrinal texts in Wahhabi and Salafi circles. Sometime in late 1298 or in 1299, a Shafiʿi judge from Wasit in Iraq asked Ibn Taymiyya to produce a creed for the Muslims in Iraq to counter a decline in Sunni religious knowledge suffered under the Mongols. Ibn Taymiyya composed a systematic account of basic theological doctrine known as the *Wasitiyya* (MF 3:129–159). According to Ibn Taymiyya's own report, the *Wasitiyya* quickly gained wide circulation in Iraq, Egypt, and beyond.

In December 1298, Ibn Taymiyya also wrote a refutation of the prevailing Ashʿari view of God's attributes for the people of the Syrian city Hama. This second treatise is known as the *Hamawiyya* (MF 5:5–120). Theologians of Ashʿari orientation were found in all Sunni law schools within the Mamluk Empire except that of the Hanbalis. Ashʿaris insisted that God should not be described with bodily attributes and human affections, and some said that scriptural texts ascribing such characteristics to God should be reinterpreted to mean something else. For example, a text ascribing a hand to God should be reinterpreted to mean that God is powerful. Ibn Taymiyya rejected such reinterpretation as distorting the plain sense of the revealed text.

This led opponents in Damascus to accuse Ibn Taymiyya of saying that God had a body (*tajsim*). The Hanafi chief judge required him to appear for a hearing. Ibn Taymiyya claimed that the Mamluk sultan had not appointed the judge to interfere in such matters, and he did not appear. The Hanafi judge responded by sending a crier to denounce Ibn Taymiyya's doctrine throughout the city. The governor of Damascus was displeased and stepped in before the crier could complete the job. Ibn Taymiyya then met with the Shafiʿi chief judge to discuss his *Hamawiyya*. The Shafiʿi supported Ibn Taymiyya and declared that anyone who speaks against him should be censured. The question of God's corporeality would return to haunt Ibn Taymiyya later, but not before the Mongols again invaded Syria.

THE MONGOL INVASION OF 1299–1300

The new Mongol threat was led by the Ilkhanid ruler Ghazan Khan. The Ilkhanid Empire had been ruled by non-Muslims for more than 35 years, but Ghazan quickly turned the tables. He converted to Sunni Islam, ascended the throne in 1295, and styled himself the Guardian of Islam. He denigrated the Mamluks and called on them to submit to his authority. The Mamluks refused, and Ghazan invaded Syria three times between 1299 and 1303. Ibn Taymiyya was skeptical of Ghazan's new-found faith, and he was eager to serve the Mamluk resistance as propagandist, diplomat, and soldier on the grounds that the Mongol invaders posed a grave danger to the integrity of Sunni Islam. The Mongol invasions also gave Ibn Taymiyya an opportunity to demonstrate his patriotism and valor while deflecting attention from his unwelcome theological views.

In July 1298, five months before the controversy over his *Hamawiyya*, Ibn Taymiyya preached jihad in the Umayyad mosque to rouse support for a Mamluk expedition to Little Armenia. Little Armenia was a Christian ally of the Mongols just to the northwest of Syria. The expedition came to nothing. A year later, in June 1299, Mamluk soldiers raided Mardin, a city in northern Mesopotamia under Mongol control. Ghazan accused the Mamluk raiders of desecrating the mosques of the city and violating its Muslim women in sexual orgies. Taking these Mamluk abominations as his pretext, Ghazan invaded Syria for the first time. He was joined by Armenian and Georgian Christian allies and Mamluk prisoners forced to fight on the Mongol side.

Ibn Taymiyya called for jihad against the Mongol invasion. Part of his argument appealed to religious patriotism. In remarks likely referring to this invasion, Ibn Taymiyya recounts how he extolled the virtues of Syria to stir the Mamluks to its defense. Syria was a divinely blessed region. It must be secured against the Mongol invaders because it is the land of the Farthest Mosque in Jerusalem and the Prophet Muhammad's Night Journey from Jerusalem into the heavens. It is also the place to which everyone will be gathered at the end of time (MF 27:505–511). In other texts Ibn Taymiyya ties the virtues of a place to the moral virtues of its inhabitants, not to characteristics of the place itself. Here Ibn Taymiyya makes an exception for the obviously pragmatic purpose of spurring the Mamluk army to fight.

Ibn Taymiyya provides further arguments for jihad in three anti-Mongol fatwas made famous by modern jihadis. The earliest of these fatwas likely dates to this first Mongol invasion (MF 28:544–553). The second fatwa dates to the second invasion of 1300–1301 or the third invasion of 1303 (MF 28:501–508). The third fatwa is the longest (MF 28:509–543); it dates to a later Mongol invasion in 1312–1313 and will be discussed in the next chapter.

The first fatwa confronts religious scruples against fighting the Mongols. Some Mamluk soldiers refused to fight because the Mongols were fellow Muslims. Ibn Taymiyya allows that the Mongols confess Islam, and he does not call them unbelievers or apostates. Nonetheless, he insists that the Mongols must be fought because they do not fully adhere to Islam. They refuse to uphold some of Islam's clear and widely accepted obligations. He roots his argument in the Qur'an: "Fight them until there is no more dissension and religion in its entirety is for God alone" (Q. 8:39) and, "O you who believe! Fear God and give up what remains of usury, if you are believers. If you do not, then be informed of war [against you] from God and His Messenger" (Q. 2:278–279). The latter Qur'an quotation, Ibn Taymiyya explains, was revealed to the Prophet Muhammad for the people of Ta'if, a town near Mecca. The people of Ta'if confessed Islam, prayed, and fasted, but they refused to abandon usury. In a similar manner, Abu Bakr, the first caliph after the Prophet died, fought Muslims who refused to pay alms. Additionally, as commanded in a statement by the Prophet Muhammad, the fourth caliph 'Ali Ibn Abi Talib, fought the rebel Kharijis for the insincerity of their religion. The Mongols, Ibn Taymiyya argues, are worse than the people of Ta'if, the Kharijis, and those who withheld alms under Abu Bakr. So it follows that they should be fought. Ibn Taymiyya says little in this first fatwa about which laws the Mongols failed to keep, but he does censure them for fighting to advance their own selfish interests and not the interests of Islam. They do not join together with other Muslims to fight the unbelievers. They fight only to establish Mongol hegemony. They are so bad that they would even stoop to fighting prophets to attain their goals.

In this first anti-Mongol fatwa, Ibn Taymiyya also considers whether the Mongols may be classified as Muslim rebels. Some of his fellow jurists would probably have preferred this classification. The paradigm case of rebels in traditional Sunni jurisprudence was the Companions of the Prophet Muhammad who rebelled against the caliphs after the Prophet's death. The Companions were those who had had contact with the Prophet during his lifetime and they enjoyed great esteem. So it was assumed that rebels among them had plausible justifications for their actions and should be regarded leniently. On that basis, later Muslim rebels with plausible justifications should be treated leniently as well.

Ibn Taymiyya will have none of this. He refuses to condone the wars between the Companions of the Prophet. Every effort should have been made to reconcile the Companions without fighting. Moreover, there is no comparison between the Mongols and rebel Companions. The Mongols are Muslims whose religion is defective. They must be fought until they purify their religion. In fact religion is the only thing worth fighting for in Ibn Taymiyya's eyes. Wars between Muslims for other reasons are inexcusable.

Ibn Taymiyya's arguments failed to achieve the desired result, at least on this occasion. Ghazan defeated the Mamluks in late December 1299 at the Battle of Wadi Khazindar between Homs and Hama. Many Mamluks were killed and others were sold to the European Christian Crusaders on Cyprus. The Mamluks had removed the last of the Crusaders from Syria and Palestine in 1291, apart from a remnant on the Lebanese coast. Panic struck Damascus, and the Shafi'i and Maliki judges fled, along with other city officials. A group of Damascene notables including Ibn Taymiyya went to visit Ghazan to plead for mercy. Ghazan took Damascus nonetheless. On January 2, 1300 (Rabi' al-thani 8, 699) Ghazan had a guarantee of security read out in the Umayyad mosque. It condemned Mamluk oppression and declared Ghazan King of Islam.

Once it was clear that the Mongols had triumphed, Ibn Taymiyya acceded to Mongol control. He could not justify a pointless fight to the death, and he worked to reduce further bloodshed. When Arjawash, the Mamluk commander of the Damascus citadel, refused to surrender, Ibn Taymiyya told him to stop resisting. He also beseeched the Mongols to release prisoners and stop their Georgian and Armenian Christian allies from devastating the countryside around Damascus. It was at this point that Ibn Taymiyya met Ghazan for a second time. According to historical chronicles, Ibn Taymiyya was only given time to pray for Ghazan. The chronicles add that he then met Mongol officials and negotiated the release of some prisoners. However, some biographies of Ibn Taymiyya provide further details to bolster his image as a heroic figure. One says that he intervened with Ghazan to procure the release of prisoners and to ward off an offer from the king of Georgia to annihilate the residents of Damascus. Another relates an anecdote that has inspired devotees of Ibn Taymiyya from his own day down to the present. He is reported to have said forthrightly to Ghazan:

> You claim to be a Muslim. You have a judge, a prayer leader, a teacher, and a prayer caller with you, according to what we have been told. Yet, you have invaded us. Your father and your grandfather Hulagu were unbelievers, and they did not do what you have done. They made a treaty and honored it, but you made a treaty and acted treacherously. You have spoken and not honored [your word]. (*Masalik* 320)

Ghazan returned home in early February 1300 and left Damascus in the hands of the Mongol army. He promised to return in the autumn to invade Egypt. After he departed, Ibn Taymiyya met the two main Mongol military leaders on separate occasions to negotiate the release of prisoners, both Muslims and non-Muslims. This gave Ibn Taymiyya an opportunity to observe the Mongols' practices and discuss religion with them. An anecdote related by Ibn Taymiyya himself may date to one of these meetings. On a visit to the Mongol camp, he told his colleagues not to forbid wine to the Mongols and the Georgians because they would be of more benefit to the Muslims drunk than sober.

Eventually, a Mamluk army approached from Egypt. The Mongols fled, and Arjawash took Damascus back for the Mamluks. Ibn Taymiyya led a campaign against taverns to eradicate wine drinking and other vices that had sprung up under the Mongols. The Mamluk army arrived in Damascus in late April 1300. They punished Mongol collaborators and installed Aqqush al-Afram as the new governor of Damascus.

The collaborator clean-up also took Ibn Taymiyya and al-Afram to Kisrawan on Mount Lebanon. The peoples of Kisrawan – Isma'ili Shi'is, Nusayris (today known as 'Alawis), Druze, and Christians – had defeated a Mamluk attempt to subdue them in 1292. Now they stood accused of helping the Mongols and the Crusaders. Ibn Taymiyya accompanied al-Afram on a raid to punish them in the summer of 1300. They surrendered to the Mamluks and agreed to pay tribute. Later, however, they revolted. The ensuing Mamluk expedition in 1305 crushed them decisively. Ibn Taymiyya supported the military action on the grounds that the peoples of Kiswaran were Shi'i heretics and collaborators with the Crusaders and the Mongols.

THE MONGOL INVASIONS OF 1300–1301 AND 1303

Ghazan was by no means finished with Syria. He launched a second invasion in late 1300 and a Crusader army on Cyprus set out to assist him. By early January 1301 the Mongols, along with Armenians and Crusaders, were terrorizing Aleppo. Ibn Taymiyya preached jihad in the Umayyad mosque. He also incited the Damascene governor al-Afram to resist the Mongols and travelled to Cairo to ask Mamluk sultan al-Nasir Muhammad Ibn Qalawun for reinforcements. Ibn Taymiyya wrote a letter to the sultan exhorting him to jihad on the grounds that the Mongols did not uphold all of the laws of Islam. This was the same argument made in his first anti-Mongol fatwa. The historian Ibn Kathir reports that Ibn Taymiyya warned the sultan in person, "If you turn away from Syria and its protection, we will raise up a sultan for it who will care for it, protect it, and develop it in secure times" (*Bidaya* 15:634). This anecdote may be an embellishment; Ibn Kathir was a student of Ibn Taymiyya's and always alert to enhancing his teacher's reputation. If the statement is credible, it appears to be the closest Ibn Taymiyya ever came to threatening rebellion against his own ruler. In the end the sultan sent troops.

The second of Ibn Taymiyya's anti-Mongol fatwas (MF 28:501–508) may date to this invasion or to the third invasion two years later.

Again, as in the first fatwa, he argues that the Mongols must be fought because they do not adhere to the laws of Islam. He also provides fuller evidence of Mongol irreligiosity. He criticizes the large number of Christians and polytheists in the Mongol camp. Few of the Mongols pray, even if they may show a certain respect toward pious Muslims. They do not fight unbelievers, and they fail to keep numerous other obligations. Instead they impose their own statutes, some of which agree with Islam and some of which do not. Most fundamentally though, as Ibn Taymiyya argued in the first fatwa, the Mongols give priority to their own Mongol cause over the interests of Islam. Following on from this, Ibn Taymiyya makes a decidedly utilitarian argument. Not fighting the Mongols would be more detrimental to the religion of Islam than fighting them. The Mongols are so evil that even immoral sinners should be rallied to fight jihad on the Mamluk side. God uses the immoral to support His religion when it is a matter of defending Islam against those who are even worse.

The second Mongol invasion ended abruptly. In the latter part of January 1301 Ghazan suddenly returned home, probably because of the harsh winter. Ibn Taymiyya himself was certain that it was due to bad weather. In a triumphalist account written immediately after the retreat, he interprets the events theologically as the repetition of a prophetic pattern. He compares the two Mongol invasions of 1299–1300 and 1300–1301 with two of the Prophet Muhammad's battles against his Meccan enemies. First, just as the early Muslims suffered loss at the Battle of Uhud in 625 because they had sinned and turned away from jihad, so also Syria fell to the first Mongol invasion in 1300 because the people had flinched from the responsibility of fighting. Second, at the Battle of the Ditch in 626–627 the early Muslims regained their resolve and God sent bitter cold and a strong wind. This wore down the enemy Meccans and sent them home. Likewise, in the winter of 1301 the Mamluks took courage and God sent snow, rain, and cold to thwart the Mongols (MF 28:424–467; *'Uqud* 120–175).

As this account and his earlier anti-Mongol writings illustrate, Ibn Taymiyya is unremitting in casting the Mamluks as the defenders of God's religion and the beneficiaries of God's providential support. As for the Mongols, they might call themselves Muslims but they are no more than a self-serving bane to religion who will receive their comeuppance. It is unthinkable to Ibn Taymiyya that the Mongols could be of any use to religion. Instead, his propaganda pulls out all the juristic stops to vilify them – apart from calling them unbelievers – and it may have played a substantive role in producing the desired result: a Mamluk state confident enough to stand up to the Mongols.

In the summer of 1301 Ghazan sent a diplomatic mission to Cairo to call on the Mamluks to submit and make peace. The Mamluks rejected the overture. They cast doubt on the authenticity of Ghazan's conversion to Islam and accused Ghazan's vassal in Mardin of provoking the abominations of 1299. They also insulted Ghazan for the paganism of his ancestors and questioned how as a Muslim he could threaten war against fellow Muslims. A further round of diplomatic exchanges in 1302 failed to soften relations between Ghazan and Mamluk sultan al-Nasir Muhammad. Neither would submit to the other.

The Syrian Mamluk army defeated Little Armenia in the summer of 1302. It also expelled the last of the Crusaders from the eastern Mediterranean coast. In the winter of 1303 Ghazan advanced into Syria for his third invasion. The Mongols approached Damascus in April and Mamluk reinforcements arrived from Egypt. Ibn Taymiyya rallied the Mamluk soldiers to fight, again rejecting worries that the Mongols should not be fought because they were Muslims. The Mamluks defeated the Mongols at Marj al-Suffar outside Damascus on April 20–22, 1303 (Ramadan 2–4, 702). Ibn Taymiyya himself bore arms in the battle. As it was the month of Ramadan, he had also produced a fatwa exempting the soldiers from fasting. A few days later, the sultan triumphantly entered Damascus. Ghazan died a year later in 1304 and was succeeded by his brother Oljeitu. The Mongols did not seriously threaten the Mamluks again until 1312, the year Oljeitu tried to invade Syria. The invasion came to nothing but it provided the occasion for Ibn Taymiyya's longest and harshest anti-Mongol fatwa. Modern-day jihadis take inspiration from Ibn Taymiyya's 1299–1303 anti-Mongol texts and activism, but it is this later fatwa that they use to justify calling their own rulers apostates. It will be discussed in the next chapter.

CHRISTIANS IN THE WAKE OF THE MONGOLS

Two of Ibn Taymiyya's better-known treatises concerning Christianity date to events in the wake of the Mongol invasions. The first involves Christians living within the Mamluk Empire. After Ghazan's unexpected retreat from Syria in January 1300, the Mamluks closed the churches in Cairo and enforced a set of laws known as the Pact of 'Umar restricting Jews and Christians. Among other things, the Pact of 'Umar dictates that Jews wear yellow turbans and Christians blue. Jews and Christians should ride donkeys rather than horses and should not be involved in the governing of Muslims. The imposition of these laws was probably retaliation for Crusader and Lebanese Christian collaboration with the Mongols. The Muslim populace of Cairo also disliked the prominence of Christians in the Mamluk bureaucracy and agitated for their removal. Many Christian bureaucrats converted to Islam. Enforcing the Pact of 'Umar was difficult, however, and things eased with time. Ibn Taymiyya supported the imposition of the Pact of 'Umar, and he wrote his treatise *The Question of the Churches* (MF 28:632–646) to argue that there was no injustice in closing the churches. Indeed, he explains, all the churches in Egypt could be destroyed if the ruler so wished because Christians resisted the original Muslim conquest of Egypt in the seventh century. Ibn Taymiyya's treatise dates to after the closing of the churches but before 1305 and was part of a broader contemporary literature arguing for harsh treatment of Christians.

The second treatise appeals for help to a Christian military official on Cyprus. Ibn Taymiyya wrote his *Cypriot Letter* (MF 28:601–636) between the Mamluk victory at Marj al-Suffar in April 1303 and the death of Ghazan in 1304. The addressee appears to be the Crusader baron John II of Giblet. The *Letter* commends Islam as the correct middle path between Christianity and Judaism. It then appeals for good treatment of Muslim prisoners on Cyprus. The Crusaders had taken Mamluk prisoners to Cyprus to hold for ransom or sell in slave markets following Ghazan's abortive second invasion, and thereafter they continued to raid the eastern coastlines of the Mediterranean for captives.

Fighting off the Mongols and cleaning up in their wake had given Ibn Taymiyya respite from the concerns of his fellow scholars over his theological doctrine, but his heroics did not win him unmitigated favor. Some were envious of his access to the corridors of power. His turn inward to fight alleged religious decay was about to make him even more enemies. That is the story for the next chapter.

2

LATER CAREER AND MAJOR TRIALS

CONFLICTS WITH SUFIS

As the Mongol threat passed, Ibn Taymiyya did not rest on his laurels. He believed that a corrupt vision of Islam had taken hold of society. Innovated rituals, spurious beliefs, and lax observance of the law had left the Muslims vulnerable to invasion, and he decided to try to stamp them out. It was a decision that would shape the rest of his career. Mention has already been made in the last chapter of his campaign against taverns in 1300 and his support for measures against churches. Opponents also complained in 1302 that he had been taking the law into his own hands by administering corporal punishments that were normally the preserve of the governing authorities.

Sufis bore the brunt of Ibn Taymiyya's activism. The Sufi spiritual path and shrine religion (i.e. practices linked to saints' tombs and sacred objects) had become integral parts of the Mamluk religious world by the late thirteenth century. Ibn Taymiyya did not regard these developments positively. The chronicler Ibn Kathir reports that the following two incidents took place in early 1305. The first involves two eccentric Sufi spiritual teachers or shaykhs, and the second a sacred rock.

> A [Sufi] shaykh named al-Mujahid Ibrahim al-Qattan, wearing a very big wide garment, was brought to Shaykh Taqi al-Din Ibn Taymiyya. [Ibn

> Taymiyya] ordered that the garment be cut up. So the people seized it from every side. They cut it until they left nothing of it. He ordered that his head be shaved because he had long hair. He cut his fingernails for they were very long. He trimmed his mustache drooping down over his mouth in violation of the Sunna [i.e. the practice of the Prophet Muhammad]. He called upon him to repent from abominable talk and from taking things that alter the mind, like hashish, unlawful things that are not permitted, and so forth. After this, he summoned Shaykh Muhammad al-Khabbaz al-Ballasi. He called upon him also to repent from taking unlawful things and mixing with the Protected Peoples [i.e. Christians and Jews]. He prescribed that he should not speak about the interpretation of dreams and other things about which he had no knowledge... Shaykh Taqi al-Din Ibn Taymiyya went to the Naranj mosque [in Damascus]. He ordered his companions and the stone cutters with them to demolish the rock that was by the Qalut River [nearby]. People used to visit it and make vows to it. So he smashed it and relieved the Muslims of it and the polytheism (*shirk*) involved in it. (*Bidaya* 16:38-39)

Another account of the rock smashing adds that the rock contained a footprint of the Prophet Muhammad and that people used to kiss it and seek blessing from it.

In late 1305 Ibn Taymiyya's conflict with a Sufi group called the Ahmadi-Rifa'is came to a head. The Ahmadi-Rifa'is were known for their music, dance, and miracle working. Ibn Taymiyya had been condemning Ahmadi-Rifa'i practices so much that they complained to the governor of Damascus. The governor summoned Ibn Taymiyya to debate with them, and he defeated them in argument. At their wits end, one of the Rifa'i shaykhs appealed to their miraculous powers, such as their ability to enter fire without suffering harm. Ibn Taymiyya challenged them to enter the fire. He demanded, however, that they first wash their bodies with vinegar and hot water to remove the flame-retardant chemicals. The Rifa'is were not willing to undergo the ordeal.

Such confrontations made Ibn Taymiyya enemies, but not enemies with sufficient power to undo him. That changed when he began to attack Ibn al-'Arabi (d. 1240), the most sophisticated Sufi theorist of medieval Islam. Ibn Taymiyya soon found himself on a collision course with much more powerful adversaries in Cairo. Sometime in late 1303 or early 1304, someone gave him Ibn al-ʿArabi's book *The Bezels of Wisdom* (*Fusus al-hikam*). *Bezels* is a work of mystical theology giving unconventional interpretations to Qur'anic stories. For example, the people who drowned in Noah's flood died in a sea of gnosis, and the Children of Israel who worshipped the calf in the wilderness were in fact worshipping God. Ibn Taymiyya found such interpretations shocking. He had read Ibn al-ʿArabi's works appreciatively before this, but *Bezels* repelled him. He wrote a number of treatises against the teachings of Ibn al-ʿArabi and his followers, including one that directly quotes and refutes parts of *Bezels* (MF 2:134–285).

Ibn Taymiyya also wrote letters of admonition to two avid and well-placed devotees of Ibn al-ʿArabi in Cairo. One was Karim al-Din al-Amuli, head of the Saʿid al-Suʿada', the leading state-sponsored Sufi lodge in Cairo. The other follower of Ibn al-ʿArabi was Nasr al-Manbiji, the spiritual director of Baybars al-Jashnakir. Baybars al-Jashnakir was chief steward to the household of Sultan al-Nasir Muhammad. The sultan was only 19 or 20 years old at the time and, because of his youth, Baybars and the sultan's viceroy Sayf al-Din Salar served together as de facto rulers of the Mamluk Empire.

The letter to al-Manbiji is extant (MF 2:452–479). Ibn Taymiyya explains that he had thought well of Ibn al-ʿArabi and had found much benefit in his works. It was not until he had read *Bezels* that he had understood Ibn al-ʿArabi's errors. To emphasize the severity of the matter, Ibn Taymiyya compares resisting Ibn al-ʿArabi and his followers to repelling the Mongols. He also makes the followers of Ibn al-ʿArabi a cause of the Mongol invasions and an apocalyptic sign: "Often I have thought that the appearance of such as these is one of the main reasons behind the appearance of the Mongols and the obliteration of the law of Islam and that these are a harbinger of the lying one-eyed Dajjal who claims to be God" (MF 2:475). (In Muslim belief the Dajjal is an evil figure who will appear near the end of history.)

Al-Manbiji was incensed. He showed Ibn Taymiyya's letter to Ibn Makhluf, the Maliki chief judge of Cairo. As in Damascus, there was one chief justice in Cairo from each of the four Sunni law schools. Maliki law prescribed death for heresy, and Ibn Makhluf was not afraid to impose it. He had already sentenced someone to death in 1301 for denigrating the divine law. Al-Manbiji was no doubt looking to Ibn Makhluf for a way to take revenge on Ibn Taymiyya. Ibn Makhluf obliged and provided him with a strategy. He advised al-Manbiji to appeal to his confidant Baybars al-Jashnakir to have Ibn Taymiyya tried on charges against his creed, specifically corporealism (*tajsim*), that is, ascribing bodily attributes to God. This was the same charge that had been leveled against Ibn Taymiyya in 1298. The Egyptian chronicler Ibn al-Dawadari reports Ibn Makhluf as saying, "It has come to my attention that [Ibn Taymiyya] has corrupted the minds of a great multitude and that he upholds *tajsim*. According to us [in the Maliki law school], whoever upholds that doctrine has disbelieved and must be killed" (*Kanz* 9:144). There was clearly worry that Ibn Taymiyya's teachings were spreading beyond the confines of the scholarly classes. The opposition to Ibn Taymiyya was not merely a matter of rivalry among scholars, as historians both medieval and modern have suggested. Substantive theological differences and competition over the beliefs of ordinary people were at the center of this conflict. Al-Manbiji took the matter to Baybars al-Jashnakir, and Sultan al-Nasir Muhammad Ibn Qalawun sent a letter to Damascus demanding that Ibn Taymiyya be tried.

THE 1306 DAMASCUS TRIALS OVER THEOLOGY

The Mamluks were not in the business of suppressing heresy through formal inquisition tribunals. However, bitter disputes over theological doctrine did break out from time to time, and the Mamluk authorities stepped in to contain and remove the sources of disturbance. In response to the sultan's letter, al-Afram, the governor of Damascus, called the four chief judges, other leading scholars, and Ibn Taymiyya to a trial on Monday, January 24, 1306 (Rajab 8, 705). Ibn Taymiyya alleged that lies had been spread about him, and he defended his theological views from his *Wasitiyya* creed written seven years earlier. Debate revolved around whether it was permissible to reinterpret revealed texts that spoke of God having bodily parts. As noted in the previous chapter, the Ash'ari theology of the day permitted this but Ibn Taymiyya did not. The governor tried to persuade Ibn Taymiyya to agree that his creed was only that of the Hanbali school and not Islam as a whole. Ibn Taymiyya refused. He insisted that his creed was that of the Salaf (the earliest Muslim generations), as well as that of all four Sunni legal schools and even the Ash'aris and Sufis.

The first trial was adjourned because it had gone on too long. The proceedings continued at a second trial four days later on Friday, January 28 (Rajab 12). Ibn Taymiyya again stood his ground. He sought to show that al-Ash'ari (d. 935), the eponym of the Ash'ari theological school, was in fact on his side and provided no support for the views of his opponents.

The sources contain different accounts of how the second trial ended. Some, like Ibn Kathir, imply that it ended well for Ibn Taymiyya, with his creed accepted as orthodox. Others, such as the Egyptian bureaucrat and chronicler al-Nuwayri, say that it ended with Ibn Taymiyya confessing to being a Shafi'i. A third account by Ibn Taymiyya's brother Sharaf al-Din accuses opponents of fabricating reports that he had retracted his creed. Ibn Taymiyya had indeed claimed that his creed was not just that of the Hanbalis but also that of the Shafi'is, the Hanafis, the Malikis, and even al-Ash'ari. This claim could have been misconstrued to mean that he had accepted the views of his Shafi'i and Ash'ari opponents. Following the trial, Shafi'i and Hanafi judges punished several of Ibn Taymiyya's followers while the governor was away on a hunting trip.

A third trial was held in Damascus on Tuesday, February 22, 1306 (Sha'ban 7, 705). Ibn Taymiyya's creed appears to have been accepted, and the trial ended in a dispute among the Shafi'is themselves.

The Damascus trials did not produce the result desired by Ibn Taymiyya's enemies in Cairo. Al-Nuwayri provides a first-hand account of what happened next. A student of religion brought a fatwa written by Ibn Taymiyya to the attention of al-Nuwayri and Ibn 'Adlan, a Shafi'i judge. The fatwa outlined the interpretation of God's attributes and the nature of God's speech. Ibn 'Adlan disliked parts of the fatwa and showed it to the Maliki chief judge Ibn Makhluf. Ibn

Makhluf verified that the fatwa was in Ibn Taymiyya's own hand, and he connived in having Ibn Taymiyya summoned to Cairo to appear before the sultan. The governor in Damascus sought to block the summons, but Ibn Makhluf again intervened. Ibn Taymiyya had to go to Cairo.

IMPRISONMENTS IN EGYPT OVER THEOLOGY AND SUFISM 1306–1310

Ibn Taymiyya arrived in Cairo on Thursday, April 7, 1306 (Ramadan 22, 705). He was tried and imprisoned with his two brothers the next day. Ibn 'Adlan brought the case before the Maliki chief judge Ibn Makhluf. Also present were Baybars al-Jashnakir and the viceroy Salar. The sultan issued a decree accusing Ibn Taymiyya of *tajsim* (corporealism) and error in the doctrine of God's speech. The decree furthermore threatened the sword for anyone who followed Ibn Taymiyya's errors. It ordered the Hanbalis, for whom it was assumed Ibn Taymiyya spoke, to retract offending doctrines or be dismissed from their posts. The decree was publicized in Syria, and Ibn Makhluf saw to it that Hanbali leaders in Cairo were persecuted.

During his first year in prison, Ibn Taymiyya set to work defending his views in two major works. The Egyptian Hanafi Shams al-Din al-Saruji had written a refutation of Ibn Taymiyya's *Hamawiyya*. Ibn Taymiyya refuted al-Saruji in a work of several volumes called *The Answer to Egyptian Objections* (*Jawab al-i'tiradat al-misriyya*). Only a small portion of this treatise is extant. Ibn Taymiyya followed with another multiple-volume tome called *Explication of the Deceit of the Jahmiyya* (*Bayan talbis al-Jahmiyya*). Ibn Taymiyya uses the name "Jahmiyya" to refer to theologians who fail to affirm the reality of God's attributes in sufficiently robust fashion. The *Explication* refutes the book *Establishing Sanctification* (*Ta'sis al-taqdis*) by the great Ash'ari theologian Fakhr al-Din al-Razi (d. 1210). The *Explication* is one of Ibn Taymiyya's longest works, and it argues that al-Razi's views on the incorporeality of God are not mainstream and do not accord with reason or revelation.

Ibn Taymiyya had sympathizers in the higher echelons of Egyptian society. After he had been in prison for a year, leading figures in Cairo sought to release him. However, he rebuffed several invitations to negotiate a compromise, including an overture by the Shafi'i chief judge Badr al-Din Ibn Jama'a. Ibn Taymiyya remained defiant in prison. He called Ibn Makhluf a liar, insisted that his creed was that of the Salaf and al-Ash'ari, and proclaimed that he did not fear death because it would make him a martyr. Eventually, the emir Husam al-Din Muhanna intervened with Sultan al-Nasir Muhammad to get Ibn Taymiyya released.

The viceroy Salar gathered a large group of scholars together with Ibn Taymiyya on Friday and Sunday, September 22 and 24, 1307 (Rabi' al-awwal 23 and 25, 707). Ibn Makhluf was ill and did not attend. None of the other chief judges attended either. A further hearing was held on October 5, 1307 (Rabi' al-thani 6, 707). Al-Nuwayri reports that on September 24 and then again on October 5 Ibn Taymiyya voluntarily signed a document that located him within the bounds of the prevailing Ash'ari orthodoxy. Other accounts indicate one signing instead of two, and al-Dhahabi reports that the wording of the document was imposed on Ibn Taymiyya under threat of death. Ibn Taymiyya had apparently decided that freedom was more suited to his broader purposes than martyrdom.

Once out of prison, Ibn Taymiyya taught and spoke against Sufis. In April 1308, the head of the Sa'id al-Su'ada' Sufi lodge, Karim al-Din al-Amuli, joined together with Ibn 'Ata' Allah al-Iskandari to lead a group of 500 Sufis to complain about Ibn Taymiyya to the viceroy Salar. Al-Amuli was one of the Sufi shaykhs to whom Ibn Taymiyya had written earlier about the dangers of Ibn al-'Arabi. Ibn 'Ata' Allah al-Iskandari was the leading figure among the Shadhili order of Sufis popular in Cairo. The order was named after the Moroccan Sufi Abu al-Hasan al-Shadhili (d. ca. 1258). Ibn Taymiyya had probably by this time composed his large *Refutation of al-Shadhili* (*al-Radd 'ala al-Shadhili*) criticizing Shadhili spiritual litanies and Ibn 'Ata' Allah had most likely taken offense.

Salar delegated the affair to the Shafi'i chief judge Badr al-Din Ibn Jama'a. Ibn Jama'a had Ibn Taymiyya debate with Ibn 'Ata' Allah, but the result was inconclusive. Finally, it was decided that Ibn Taymiyya should return to Syria. However, Ibn Makhluf, who was gravely ill, heard of Ibn Taymiyya's departure and had Salar bring him back to Cairo. One Maliki deputy judge would not sentence Ibn Taymiyya to prison. A second Maliki judge was not sure what to do. So Ibn Taymiyya said that he would go back to prison for the sake of the public good. He was imprisoned in Cairo on Friday, April 12, 1308 (Shawwal 19, 707) and remained there for 16 months, writing and receiving visitors.

According to his biographer Ibn 'Abd al-Hadi, Ibn Taymiyya kindled a religious revival in prison. Ibn 'Abd al-Hadi's report illustrates Ibn Taymiyya's forceful and charismatic personality, and it no doubt captures in miniature the religious reform that Ibn Taymiyya wished to see in the wider society:

> When he entered prison, he found the prisoners busy whiling away the time with various kinds of games such as chess, backgammon, and such like that lead to neglecting ritual prayers. The shaykh rebuked them for that in the strongest of terms and commanded them to perform the ritual prayer and turn to God with righteous deeds, glorification, seeking forgiveness, and supplication. He taught them what they needed to know of the Sunna [of the Prophet]. He roused them to perform good deeds and spurred them on. Busy with learning and religion, the prison turned out to be better than [Sufi] prayer rooms and hospices, [Sufi] lodges, and religious schools. When prisoners were released, many of them chose to remain by his side. The number of people who frequented him increased to the point that the prison was full of them. (*'Uqud* 269)

Back on the political front, Sultan al-Nasir Muhammad, now into his early 20s, schemed to displace his chief steward Baybars al-Jashnakir and his viceroy Salar as de facto rulers but was not successful. So in March 1309 he moved to Kerak to the east of the Dead Sea and abdicated the throne. Salar allowed Baybars to take the throne to avoid conflict. Baybars became sultan and appointed Salar as his viceroy. Ibn Taymiyya was not impressed with the political changes. He criticized Baybars, his spiritual guide Nasr al-Din al-Manbiji, and Ibn al-'Arabi. Ibn Kathir reports that Ibn Taymiyya spoke dismissively of Baybars: "His days have passed; his leadership has come to an end; and the end of his time has drawn near" (*Bidaya* 16:69). In August 1309 Baybars transferred Ibn Taymiyya to Alexandria, where he was put under house arrest for eight months but continued to teach and write.

Ibn Taymiyya's book *Rectitude* (*al-Istiqama*) dates to approximately this time. Much of *Rectitude* is devoted to discussion of *The Treatise* (*al-Risala*) of Abu al-Qasim al-Qushayri (d. 1073), who was both a Sufi and an Ash'ari theologian. Ibn Taymiyya critiques al-Qushayri's views on theology and the Sufi practice of using music to aid worship. *Rectitude* includes a long discussion of the Qur'anic ethical injunction to "command the right and prohibit the wrong." This discussion was appended to his later work *Public Morals* (*al-Hisba*), and it also exists as an independent treatise.

FINAL YEARS IN EGYPT 1310–1313

Baybars al-Jashnakir struggled to stay in power. The more popular al-Nasir Muhammad returned as sultan in March 1310 and reigned until his death in 1341. Baybars was executed and Salar was starved to death. It seems that al-Nasir Muhammad had a certain admiration for Ibn Taymiyya. The sultan brought him back to Cairo from Alexandria and honored him before an audience of judges and scholars from both Egypt and Syria. He also quelled Ibn Makhluf's enmity toward Ibn Taymiyya. Ibn 'Abd al-Hadi reports that Ibn Taymiyya turned down an offer from al-Nasir Muhammad to have his enemies put to death. Ibn Makhluf then responded, "I have not seen anyone more pious than Ibn Taymiyya. We can no longer seek to destroy him. When he gets the better of us, he pardons us" (*'Uqud* 282–283). Ibn Taymiyya's fortunes had clearly improved, and he enjoyed a period of relative calm before returning to Damascus in 1313.

A number of Ibn Taymiyya's better-known works date to his final years in Egypt. He appears to have drafted his famous *Law-Guided Public Policy* (*al-Siyasa al-shar'iyya*) around 1310 and completed it after returning to Damascus. The book outlines the responsibilities of those in positions of leadership – both rulers and scholars – to improve the religious and ethical condition of society. I will survey the contents of this book in Chapter Six. In 1311 or 1312 Ibn Taymiyya wrote a treatise explaining that seeking access to God (*tawassul*) is through obedience to the Prophet, not through the Prophet himself (MF 1:313–368). The argument is typical of Ibn Taymiyya's ethicized religion of obedience. The Sufi Nur al-Din Bakri responded with a book that supported seeking aid directly from prophets and the dead. Ibn Taymiyya countered with his own book *Seeking Aid in the Refutation of al-Bakri* (*Al-Istighatha fi radd 'ala al-Bakri*). Occasionally Ibn Taymiyya also tried his hand at poetry, although he was not known to be particularly good at it. Composing poetry was an important way of demonstrating virtuosity in Mamluk scholarly circles. Ibn Taymiyya's longest poem, comprising 124 verses against fatalism in response to a question from an alleged non-Muslim (MF 8:245–255), has been dated to 1312. The questioner was very likely a Muslim with Shi'i tendencies, and five other Cairene scholars also responded in verse. In 1312 or 1313 Ibn Taymiyya composed a commentary on the creed of Shams al-Din Muhammad Ibn Mahmud al-Isfahani (d. 1289), a follower of the Ash'ari theologian Fakhr al-Din al-Razi. Another work, his lengthy critique of popular religious practices called *The Necessity of the Straight Path* (*Iqtida' al-sirat al-mustaqim*), may also date to his time in Egypt, or perhaps to his first two years back in Damascus. Its earliest extant manuscript is dated 1315.

Ibn Taymiyya's later years in Egypt also witnessed renewed hostility from the Mongols. The Ilkhanid ruler Oljeitu converted from Sunnism to Twelver Shi'ism in 1309, and he marched on Syria in 1312. The longest of Ibn Taymiyya's three famous anti-Mongol fatwas contains an allusion to Oljeitu's conversion to Shi'ism, and he probably wrote the fatwa in Egypt at this point to address the new Mongol threat. The fatwa expands and makes harsher the argument of the two earlier fatwas. As before, the Mongols must be fought because they are worse than the Kharijis and those who withheld alms from the first caliph Abu Bakr. Ibn Taymiyya then goes into much greater detail about the defectiveness of the Mongols' Islam. They are lax in their religious practices. They corrupt true religion with Shi'ism and errant Sufism. They still use their old Mongol legal code called the *yasa*. They regard the different religions like Judaism, Christianity, and Islam as equally valid paths to God. Ibn Taymiyya also calls those who withheld alms from Abu Bakr apostates, something that he did not do in the first two fatwas. He accuses the Mongols of being even worse because they fight Muslims. If the Mongols were to conquer Syria and Egypt, he claims, the religion of Islam would disappear (MF 28:509–543).

Ibn Taymiyya's opinion of the Mongols had hardened with time. He had not called them apostates or even unbelievers during the invasions of 1299 to 1303. Modern-day jihadis use this later anti-Mongol fatwa to justify calling those who do not uphold Islamic law as they see fit unbelievers and apostates, even the Muslim rulers of their own countries. Ibn Taymiyya himself never called his Mamluk rulers apostates. Even though they fell far short of Ibn Taymiyya's Islamic ideals, they sufficed to serve as the protectors of Sunni Islam.

As it turned out, the Mongol threat passed quickly. In early 1313, Mamluk Sultan al-Nasir Muhammad and his army set out to fight the Mongols. Ibn Taymiyya and his brothers and comrades joined the expedition, but the Mongols turned back without a fight. Ibn Taymiyya and his travelling companions separated from the Mamluk army, visited Jerusalem, and then returned permanently to Damascus. The Mongols and Mamluks eventually signed a treaty, and the Mamluk Empire settled into a period of peace and prosperity.

BACK IN DAMASCUS TEACHING AND WRITING

Ibn Taymiyya was well received in Damascus upon his arrival in late February 1313. He returned to his teaching posts at the Sukkariyya and Hanbaliyya madrasas, and he gained new followers including his leading disciple Ibn Qayyim al-Jawziyya, or Ibn al-Qayyim for short. Ibn Taymiyya now wrote even more extensively. Spurred on by his trials in Egypt, he elaborated his unique theological views over against the prevailing theologies and philosophies of the day, especially the Ash'arism of Fakhr al-Din al-Razi and the philosophy of Avicenna (d. 1037, known as Ibn Sina in Arabic). Chapters Seven and Eight will outline Ibn Taymiyya's theology more systematically. Here I will note the major theological works that Ibn Taymiyya wrote once back in Damascus.

Ibn Taymiyya's masterwork *Averting the Conflict between Reason and Revealed Tradition* (*Dar' ta'arud al-'aql wa al-naql*) dates to sometime after 1313 and comes to eleven volumes in the published edition. In this tome Ibn Taymiyya refutes claims to rationality made by Muslim theologians and philosophers, and sets forth his own vision of a true rationality that accords with divine revelation. More will be said about this work in Chapter Seven. Ibn Taymiyya had begun work on his *Refutation of the Logicians* (*al-Radd 'ala al-mantiqiyyin*) during his imprisonment in Alexandria in 1309–1310 and then completed it in Damascus. The *Refutation* criticizes Aristotelian logic and its notions of definition and certain knowledge. It also reveals Ibn Taymiyya's faulty understanding of the standard logical doctrines of his day. Ibn Taymiyya wrote his large work *Safadiyya*, named after the town of Safad in northern Palestine, while working on *Averting the Conflict* and the *Refutation of Logic*. *Safadiyya* refutes naturalistic interpretations of miracles.

Ibn Taymiyya completed his extensive *Way of the Sunna* (*Minhaj al-sunna*) after finishing *Averting the Conflict*. *The Way of the Sunna* is a line-by-line refutation of *The Way of Nobility* (*Minhaj al-karama*), an apologetic for Twelver Shi'ism by the prominent Shi'i scholar Ibn al-Mutahhar al-Hilli (d. 1325). Al-Hilli maintains that the Prophet Muhammad designated his cousin and son-in-law 'Ali as the first leader (*imam*) of the Muslim community, whereas Ibn Taymiyya defends the Sunni doctrine that 'Ali was preceded by three others: Abu Bakr, 'Umar, and 'Uthman. Al-Hilli also argues for the superior knowledge, piety, and status of the twelve Shi'i *imams* from 'Ali onward. Ibn Taymiyya rejects the divine prerogatives that Shi'is ascribe to their *imams*, and he contends that 'Ali was surpassed by others in knowledge of some subjects and that Abu Bakr was more pious than 'Ali.

Ibn Taymiyya's *Correct Answer* (*al-Jawab al-sahih*) is the longest refutation of Christian doctrine in the Islamic tradition. It dates to 1316 or shortly thereafter. The work argues that Christianity is both irrational and a deviation from the true religion of Christ. Ibn Taymiyya's large

Prophetic Matters (*Nubuwwat*) dates to no earlier than 1316 and was probably written several years later. In dialogue with Ash'ari theology and Avicennan philosophy, the book establishes the criteria by which to recognize a true prophet. Fuller descriptions of the *Correct Answer* and *Prophetic Matters* will be provided in Chapter Eight.

THE 1318 NUSAYRI REVOLT

The year 1318 saw Ibn Taymiyya again taking a stronger stance in the public sphere. In early 1318, the Nusayris – today called 'Alawis – of the Jabala region on the Mediterranean coast of Syria revolted in response to Mamluk attempts to rationalize taxation and religious affairs. The Nusayris did not pray in mosques and held beliefs at odds with Sunni Islam. The Mamluks had earlier tried to subdue the Nusayris, but with minimal success. Ibn Taymiyya wrote three fatwas against the Nusayris. The longest may date to 1305 but is more likely to refer to the 1318 Nusayri uprising (MF 35:145–160). A very short fatwa declares both the Druze and the Nusayris unbelievers and apostates (MF 35:161–162). The date of this fatwa is not known, and the reference to the Druze may have been added by a later hand. The third fatwa is also short and responds directly to the 1318 uprising (FK 3:513–514).

Ibn Taymiyya was the only scholar in medieval Islam to write against the Nusayris. Not much was known about them at the time and Ibn Taymiyya confuses their beliefs and practices with those of the Isma'ili Shi'is. He declares the Nusayris apostates who may be killed and whose property may be confiscated. They are to be fought with jihad until they obey the laws of Islam. Their leaders are to be killed even if they repent. Ibn Taymiyya may have been excessively harsh in order to stir the Mamluks against the Nusayris for his own religious ends. Apart from the 1318 uprising, taxes on Nusayri agriculture provided the Mamluks with a source of revenue, and the Nusayris had assisted them against the Mongols. The Mamluks spared the Nusayris in the end, but Ibn Taymiyya's anti-Nusayri fatwas echo down to the present in extremist Sunni polemic against the 'Alawis and the Druze in Syria.

TRIALS OVER DIVORCE OATHS

Ibn Taymiyya also endured trials over divorce oaths in 1318. Divorce played a key role in the fabric of Mamluk society. Mamluk officials solidified their social commitments and their loyalty to the sultan by oaths on pain of triple divorce. Such oaths were used in the courts and the marketplaces as well. Triple divorce meant issuing three divorce pronouncements at one time, which dissolved a marriage irrevocably. The woman had to marry another man (*muhallil*) and be divorced from him before she could return to her first husband. A man who broke his oath on pain of triple divorce and wished to reunite with his wife had to suffer the humiliation of first losing her to another man.

In the spring of 1318 or perhaps a little earlier, Ibn Taymiyya wrote a short critique of oaths on pain of divorce called *The Meeting and the Parting* (MF 33:44–57). Breaking with his own earlier opinion, Ibn Taymiyya argues that violation of an oath on pain of divorce does not result in an actual divorce. The man's intention is to underline the solemnity of his oath, not to divorce his wife in fact. The penalty for violating a divorce oath is the same as that for violating other kinds of oaths: an act of expiation, such as feeding the poor. In other texts, Ibn Taymiyya further deflates the force of oaths on pain of triple divorce by rejecting the validity of triple divorce itself. As I will detail in Chapter Five, three pronouncements at once count as one pronouncement only, and the man may return to his wife without her first having to marry and divorce another man. Even if violation of an oath on pain of triple divorce were to result in an actual divorce, it would not be irrevocable.

Ibn Taymiyya's views struck at the heart of Mamluk authority structures and circumvented the consensus of all four Sunni law schools. A man who broke his oath on pain of triple divorce would no longer lose his wife. If Ibn Taymiyya's opinion were to prevail, a man's oath of allegiance to the sultan would be effectively dissolved.

In June 1318 a group of leading religious scholars in Damascus met to ask the Hanbali chief judge to admonish Ibn Taymiyya. The Hanbali judge followed through, and Ibn Taymiyya agreed to stop issuing fatwas on divorce oaths. A month later a royal edict arrived in Damascus from Cairo prohibiting Ibn Taymiyya from issuing divorce oath fatwas. The edict also called for a hearing on the matter. The hearing was held and the prohibition against Ibn Taymiyya was announced publicly. It appears that he complied, at least for a while.

Eventually, however, Ibn Taymiyya returned to speaking and writing about divorce oaths. He said that he could not withhold knowledge. In November 1319 a group of judges and jurists met with the governor of Damascus. A letter from the sultan in Cairo was read, which included a section once more prohibiting Ibn Taymiyya from pronouncing on divorce oaths. The following year, in August 1320, Ibn Taymiyya was yet again brought before a hearing of leading state and religious authorities in Damascus. He was reprimanded for continuing to speak about divorce issues. He was also ordered to sign a document agreeing to stop giving fatwas on divorce. It appears that he did so. Nonetheless, Ibn Taymiyya was imprisoned in the citadel of Damascus for five and a half months. The sultan then issued a decree in February 1321 that he be released, and he returned to his house.

Foremost among the jurists who opposed Ibn Taymiyya on divorce was the Egyptian Shafi'i jurist Taqi al-Din al-Subki. Al-Subki completed a refutation of Ibn Taymiyya's *The Meeting and the Parting* in November 1318 and wrote a number of other refutations of his views on divorce. Against Ibn Taymiyya, al-Subki insisted that an oath on pain of divorce results in an actual divorce when the oath is violated. Al-Subki also charged Ibn Taymiyya with violating the firm consensus of the Muslim community on rulings pertaining to divorce itself. Ibn Taymiyya eventually responded to al-Subki with his extensive *Refutation of al-Subki on the Question of Conditional Divorce* (*Al-Radd 'ala al-Subki fi mas'alat ta'liq al-talaq*). The first part of this work has been lost.

Throughout the ordeal over divorce oaths, Ibn Taymiyya clearly found it difficult to obey the authorities. Yet he did attempt to comply, if only for the sake of public decorum. As in his trials over God's attributes, it appears that Ibn Taymiyya sought to balance the ideals of his religious vision with the limitations of the political and social realities of the moment. He might test the limits of what his society would bear, but he would not induce chaos or instigate his own execution.

FINAL IMPRISONMENT OVER GRAVE VISITATION 1326–1328

When he was released from prison in 1321 Ibn Taymiyya went back to teaching and writing. He would suffer further trials beginning in mid-1326, but the chroniclers and biographers have little to say about him in the intervening years. Ibn Kathir does state that in February 1326 Ibn Taymiyya and the leading scholars and public figures of Damascus attended the execution of a certain Nasir Ibn Sharaf, who was charged with unbelief and heresy. Ibn Kathir was present as well. He recalls seeing Ibn Taymiyya go up to Nasir Ibn Sharaf and strike him just before he was beheaded. Ibn Taymiyya's zeal against irreligion did not slacken with age.

The sources also tell us that Ibn Taymiyya met regularly with the erudite Ash'ari theologian Mahmud Ibn 'Abd al-Rahman al-Isfahani from 1325 onward. Al-Isfahani had risen to scholarly prominence in Tabriz, the great intellectual center of the Ilkhan Mongol Empire. He moved to Damascus in early 1325 and then to Cairo in 1332, where he died in 1348. Ibn Kathir reports that al-Isfahani often visited Ibn Taymiyya and studied his works with him, including the latter's criticism of the theologians. The regard may have been mutual. The biographical dictionary of Ibn Hajar al-'Asqalani, who wrote a century later, relates that Ibn Taymiyya attended al-Isfahani's lectures and held him in high esteem.

The zeal of Ibn Taymiyya's disciples Shihab al-Din Ibn Murri and Ibn Qayyim al-Jawziyya paved the way for his final trials. Ibn Taymiyya himself had been shrewd enough to survive the political hazards of Mamluk society thus far, but he does not seem to have reckoned adequately with the rashness of his followers. In the spring of 1325, Ibn Murri provoked an uproar among Sufis in Cairo by promoting the doctrines of his teacher against grave visitation and intercession through the Prophet. The Sufis complained to the Maliki chief judge Taqi al-Din al-Ikhna'i, who had Ibn Murri put into prison. Al-Ikhna'i then brought Ibn Murri to the sultan for a hearing before the chief judges and other public officials. Al-Ikhna'i may have pressed for the death penalty. However, some at the hearing supported Ibn Murri, including the Shafi'i chief judge Badr al-Din Ibn Jama'a. A fierce dispute ensued. The sultan washed his hands of the matter by delegating it to his deputy. The deputy also made no effort to resolve the case and turned it back over to al-Ikhna'i. Al-Ikhna'i imprisoned Ibn Murri and beat him. After someone intervened on behalf of Ibn Murri, it was agreed that he should be released from prison and banished from Cairo. He eventually found his way to Damascus.

The following year, Ibn al-Qayyim preached in Jerusalem against setting out to travel solely for the purpose of visiting the graves of prophets and the righteous. He announced that he would not visit the nearby grave of Abraham. Jerusalem at the time was a prosperous pilgrimage destination and his views threatened the economic and religious interests of those involved in pilgrimage operations. He was interrogated in Nablus, where it was reported that he had said the grave of the Prophet Muhammad in Medina was not to be visited at all.

Word of Ibn al-Qayyim's assertions reached Damascus, and a number of Maliki and Shafi'i jurists issued a fatwa against Ibn Taymiyya, the alleged source of his student's controversial views. They accused Ibn Taymiyya of being the first to speak out against visiting graves and charged him with unbelief. Ibn 'Abd al-Hadi writes that they based their charge on a fatwa (MF 27:183–192) that Ibn Taymiyya had written about 17 years earlier. The jurists gave their own response fatwa to the governor of Damascus and he sent it to Sultan al-Nasir Muhammad in Cairo. The sultan called a meeting of the judges. The Shafi'i chief judge Badr al-Din Ibn Jama'a declared Ibn Taymiyya misguided. It was decided to have him imprisoned and his right to issue fatwas revoked. This stands in contrast to the earlier treatment of Ibn Murri. The sultan had been indecisive over Ibn Murri, and Ibn Jama'a had even supported him. Now, though, the sultan and Ibn Jama'a joined hands against Ibn Taymiyya to contain the fallout from his ideas.

The sultan's decree arrived in Damascus on Monday, July 8, 1326 (Sha'ban 6, 726). Ibn Taymiyya was imprisoned in the citadel that same afternoon. His brother Zayn al-Din was permitted to accompany him to attend to his needs. The sultan's decree was read out in the Umayyad mosque on Friday, July 12 (Sha'ban 10). The following Wednesday, the Shafi'i chief judge, with the blessing of the governor, imprisoned a number of Ibn Taymiyya's comrades, including Ibn al-Qayyim. Some were interrogated, charged with heresies, whipped, and returned to prison. Ibn al-Qayyim was whipped as well and paraded around the city on a donkey. Ibn Taymiyya's colleagues were soon released, but Ibn al-Qayyim was released only after his teacher's death more than two years later.

Back in Cairo, the Maliki chief judge al-Ikhna'i raised the stakes by writing a refutation of Ibn Taymiyya accusing him of forbidding travel to visit the grave of the Prophet Muhammad. Ibn Taymiyya responded from prison in Damascus with a lengthy and scathing refutation known as the *Ikhna'iyya*. He accuses the Maliki judge of ignorance in religion and concocting lies and asserts that his own books are in fact full of recommendations to visit graves. He only condemns travel to graves that is undertaken solely or primarily for the purpose of visiting them. Graves may be visited only in conjunction with travel undertaken for other purposes such as visiting the mosque of the Prophet in Medina.

Ibn Taymiyya's refutation angered al-Ikhna'i, who complained to the sultan. The sultan had now had enough of Ibn Taymiyya, and the punishment was severe. On Monday, May 1, 1328 (Jumada al-thaniya 19, 728), Ibn Taymiyya was deprived of his pen, ink, and paper. He was forbidden to read and write, and his books were removed to storage. Ibn 'Abd al-Hadi tells us that Ibn Taymiyya's last writings were letters to his colleagues scratched out with charcoal.

In one of these letters, which Ibn 'Abd al-Hadi transcribes, Ibn Taymiyya remains firm in his conviction that he is fighting for the truth. He explains that his refutation of al-Ikhna'i had made his opponents nervous. God then incited them to try to concoct arguments against him. They found this exceedingly difficult, and it brought them up against their own ignorance and deceitfulness in a way that only God could effect. So to get what they wanted, they resorted for help to a creature, namely, the sultan. But, scolds Ibn Taymiyya, no creature may be obeyed in disobedience to God. At the end of the letter, Ibn Taymiyya recasts his battle in terms of jihad. His jihad against error in grave visitation is similar to his jihads against the Mongols, the people of Kisrawan, the Ash'aris, and Ibn al-'Arabi-inspired Sufis. His whole career in its diverse aspects had been a jihad for the sake of

God. He concludes, "That is the greatest of the blessings of God to us and the people, but most people do not know it" (*'Uqud* 363–364). The Mamluk state and its religious authorities may have silenced Ibn Taymiyya's public voice for good, but they had not crushed his spirit.

Ibn Taymiyya devoted his last five months of life to worship and recitation of the Qur'an. He died on Monday, September 26, 1328 (Dhu Qa'da 20, 728) in the citadel of Damascus after a short illness. Ibn Kathir, following the Syrian historian al-Birzali, reports that his body was washed and taken to the Umayyad congregational mosque for the funeral prayer accompanied by great crowds anxious to demonstrate their devotion. Al-Birzali gives generous estimates of some 15,000 women and more than 60,000 men streaming into the streets. Ibn Taymiyya was then buried in the Sufi cemetery to the west of the walled city of Damascus next to his brother Sharaf al-Din, who had died the year before.

3

THE PRIORITY OF WORSHIP

Ibn Taymiyya fought much of his jihad with the pen, and it is to a presentation of his religious thought that we turn in this and the following five chapters. One of the first things that confronts readers of Ibn Taymiyya is the diffuse and ad hoc character of his writings. He did not compose large systematic manuals of theology, legal theory, substantive law, or spiritual practice, and he never wrote a verse-by-verse commentary on the Qur'an. Instead, Ibn Taymiyya wrote to meet the needs of the moment. He responded directly to the controversies and concerns of his time in hundreds of fatwas, treatises, and books. He adopted the terminology of the questions that he was discussing or the texts that he was refuting. He shifted registers of language according to his audience and purpose.

Given the nature of Ibn Taymiyya's writing, it is not always easy to correlate what he says in one place with what he writes in another. His works often cannot be dated with sufficient precision to postulate change and development in his thought. Additionally, Ibn Taymiyya tests the patience of readers with long digressions from one apparently unrelated topic to another. There are long lists of names and pages upon pages filled with quotations from the Qur'an, the sayings and deeds of the Prophet Muhammad, and the books of earlier scholars. It can be tempting to conclude that Ibn Taymiyya was not an orderly and coherent thinker.

Yet sustained attention to Ibn Taymiyya's corpus bears out the fact that he has a distinctive message. Certain themes and patterns of thought recur, and his writings display a consistency of purpose and intention. He does clothe his ideas in a vast array of terms, and he expresses them in varying degrees of complexity and technical rigor. It is in fact Ibn Taymiyya's conviction that words do not have literal or fixed meanings.

Contrary to much that has been written about him, he is not a literalist. The meanings of words depend on the different contexts in which they are used. It is thus possible to say the same thing in many different ways. Digressions are not necessarily digressions, but simply means of thinking about the questions at hand from other perspectives or observing how similar questions emerge in other issues. The ideas are consistent and interconnected, but the expression takes ever new forms like the changing patterns of colored glass in a kaleidoscope.

The presentation of Ibn Taymiyya's thought that follows will start with worship, a term that is often synonymous in his writings with love and obedience, and is closely linked to God's law, command, and divinity. By whatever name, worship is at the heart of Ibn Taymiyya's vision. Worship is the driving force behind his efforts to articulate and promote the version of Islam that he holds to be true and that he believes to be of ultimate benefit to humanity. However the kaleidoscope turns, worship is shaping the mosaic pattern.

WORSHIP AND THE HUMAN NATURAL CONSTITUTION

Ibn Taymiyya writes, "The entirety of the religion has two principles: that we worship God alone, and that we worship Him only by means of what He has legislated. We do not worship Him by means of innovations" (MF 10:234). On Ibn Taymiyya's interpretation, these two principles correspond to the two halves of the Muslim confession of faith, "There is no god but God, and Muhammad is the Messenger of God." "There is no god but God" means that God alone is to be worshipped, and "Muhammad is the Messenger of God" means that God is to be worshipped only by means of the law revealed to the Prophet Muhammad. This gives both halves of the confession a highly ethical coloring. They are not merely statements of belief but calls for action.

Ethical interpretation of the first half of the confession goes against the grain of Ibn Taymiyya's theological context. Interpretations of "There is no god but God" dominant in his day were metaphysical and ontological. They had to do with the nature of what exists. Some

Sufis understood "There is no god but God" in one sense to mean that nothing ultimately exists at all except God. Ibn Taymiyya rejects this because it denies the concrete reality of the created world. The Ash'ari theologians interpreted "There is no god but God" to affirm the existence of only one God, the unity of this God's essence, and the uniqueness of this God as creator of the universe. Ibn Taymiyya by no means denies these senses of God's oneness, but he takes a distinctively ethical turn by locating the principal meaning of the confession in the realm of human action. "There is no god but God" signifies that no one other than God is to be worshipped and obeyed. God's unique right to be worshipped is primary, and the other senses of God's oneness follow on from this. Ethics comes first, ontology second. Interpretation of "There is no god but God" as worship of God alone finds strong precedents in Sufi theology and the Qur'an (9:31) and, following Ibn Taymiyya, it has become the primary meaning of the first half of the Islamic confession for Wahhabis, Salafis, and many reform-minded Muslims today.

Ethical interpretation of the second half of the Muslim confession of faith was less controversial. Ash'ari theologians and others also understood "Muhammad is the Messenger of God" to mean that the Prophet Muhammad had brought a revealed law that was to be obeyed. Nevertheless, there was still disagreement over what following the Prophet meant in practice. Ibn Taymiyya especially criticizes Sufis for undermining obedience to God's law with esotericism and elitism, as well as for promoting innovative practices not supported by the law. I will address some of these practices in the next chapter.

Ibn Taymiyya also links his two principles of worship to what it means to be human, to what it means to be a creature created by God. For Ibn Taymiyya human nature is dynamic and goal-oriented. Every living being has a motive force, a spirituality, a life energy, which Ibn Taymiyya calls love, worship, obedience, and will. This life energy is always oriented toward some end. It cannot escape having a goal. It also necessarily follows a path or a pattern of life as it moves toward that goal. The proper end of this vital force is God, and the proper path is the law of Islam. Ibn Taymiyya elaborates:

> Every living being must have an object of love, which is the goal of its love and its will and towards which its inner and outer movements are directed.

> That is its god. That [love, will, and movement] is of no benefit unless it is for God alone, without giving Him an associate. Everything other than Islam is worthless… Every religion, obedience, and love must have two things. The first is the object of religion, love, and obedience. This is the object of intention and the object of will. The second is the form of the deeds by which [that object] is obeyed and worshipped. This is the way, the path, the law, the method, and the means of access… Religion encompasses two things: the object of worship and the worship. The object of worship is the one God. Worship is obeying Him and obeying His Messenger. This is the religion of God with which He is well pleased. As He said, "I am well pleased with Islam as a religion for you" (Q. 5:3). (*Mahabba* 39–40)

This text affirms that love, worship, religion, and obedience are the very essence of life. Ibn Taymiyya does not confine love, worship, and religion to the private sphere. Living beings necessarily love and worship something in everything they do. The question is not whether they will worship, love, and obey. It is what they will worship and how. For Ibn Taymiyya, God is the only beneficial object of worship, and Islam is the correct method to express it. These are Ibn Taymiyya's two principles of religion: worship of God alone and worship by means of God's law.

Furthermore, Ibn Taymiyya explains why God created living beings in the way that He did. God wanted worshippers. God brought human beings and their invisible counterparts the jinn (i.e. genies) into existence so that they might devote their entire life energies to Him: "I have not created the jinn and human beings except to worship Me" (Q. 51:56). Moreover, Ibn Tayymiyya argues, God created human beings to love and worship God naturally. He supports this with a famous saying from the Prophet Muhammad: "Every newborn is born with the natural constitution (*fitra*). Then, his parents make him a Jew, Christian or Zoroastrian. This is like an animal that bears another that is perfect of limb. Do you sense any mutilation in it? Then Abu Hurayra said: If you wish, recite, 'The natural constitution of God according to which He has constituted humanity'" (Q. 30:30).

Some Muslim scholars have interpreted the natural constitution to be knowledge of Islam or predestination to Paradise and Hell. For others, it is birth into Islam or a state of moral neutrality. Ibn Taymiyya broadens the meaning of natural constitution beyond any one of these earlier interpretations, in a strongly ethical direction. The natural constitution is not only knowledge of God and birth into Islam. It is also a strong moral instinct. It is even stronger than the instincts of infants to drink their mothers' milk. God has naturally constituted human beings to love and worship only Him, and they will do so if left unhindered by impediments such as Jewish, Christian, or Zoroastrian parents. Human beings will naturally do what is right and just and avoid what is wrong and unjust. They will seek what is profitable and pleasurable, and they will repel what is harmful and painful. They will worship God by obeying his commands and prohibitions, loving what He loves, and hating what He hates.

Ibn Taymiyya is obviously very optimistic about the positive inclinations of the human natural constitution. It might even appear that prophets are no longer necessary. It looks as if humans can find their way to God on their own. In response to such concerns, Ibn Taymiyya clarifies that the task of prophets is to complete and perfect the natural constitution. He speaks with similar optimism about the powers of reason. Reason knows that God exists and that worship should be devoted to God alone. Moreover, reason knows right from wrong, pleasure from pain, and benefit from detriment. As with the natural constitution, prophecy does not oppose reason but confirms and completes it.

A SPIRITUALITY OF LOVE

Ibn Taymiyya often uses love (*mahabba*) as a synonym for worship (*'ibada*). Both terms point to that fundamental human vitality or spirituality that finds its sole end in God and its proper expression in obedience to God's law. Loving and worshipping anything other than God is associating a partner with God (*shirk*). It is idolatry and polytheism, which is the gravest sin in Islam: "God does not forgive associating [partners] with Him. He forgives less than that to whomever He wills" (Q. 4:48).

Yet the Qur'an and the sayings of the Prophet clearly countenance other loves beyond love of God. The following Qur'anic verse speaks of love for the Messenger Muhammad: "Say! If your fathers, your sons, your brothers, your wives, your relatives, wealth you have obtained, business that you fear will decline, and houses in which you take satisfaction are more beloved to you than God, His Messenger, and striving in His way, then wait until God comes with His command [of punishment]" (Q. 9:24). The following saying of the Prophet links sweetness of faith to love of God and the Messenger and a properly focused love for other human beings: "Whoever has three [characteristics] will find sweetness of faith in his heart: the one to whom God and His Messenger are more beloved than any other; the one who loves someone but loves him only for the sake of God; and the one who hates to return to unbelief after God saved him from it just as he hates to be thrown into Hell-Fire." Other sayings of the Prophet exhort love for the Prophet's Companions, that is, those who had had direct contact with Muhammad.

How is one to love God alone and yet also love the Prophet Muhammad and others? Ibn Taymiyya clarifies that there is a difference between loving a creature *for* God and loving a creature *together with* God. In loving a creature for God, God remains the final object of love and worship. The Prophet and God's righteous servants are then loved because God Himself loves them. Just as worship of God alone involves worshipping Him by means of His law, so also love for God leads to loving what God loves and loving those whom God loves. Nothing may be loved for its own sake apart from God. Loving a creature together with God is loving someone in competition with God and in disobedience to God. This includes turning to intercessors apart from God and loving and obeying human authorities, such as Sufi shaykhs, religious scholars, and rulers, at the expense of God.

Ibn Taymiyya complains that some scholars interpret love of God as merely love of obeying God or love of drawing close to Him. He singles out the Ash'ari theologian al-Juwayni (d. 1085) for denying that humans can love God in Himself. Ibn Taymiyya counters that love of drawing close to God is a consequence of loving God for His own sake. One has to love something in itself in order to love drawing close to it. Drawing close to God is a means of access to God, not an end in itself. Likewise, obedience and worship of God follow on from love of God for Himself, not out of love for obedience and worship on their own. Anyone who works for someone only to earn reward or avoid punishment does not love that person.

Ibn Taymiyya devotes considerable attention to the correct channeling of the human energy that is love. This flows from his concern for his second principle of religion, worshipping God by means of God's law. Ibn Taymiyya counsels moderation in food, drink, and sex, which are necessary for the health of the body and continuation of the human race. He warns especially against passionate love (*'ishq*), which is excessive love directed to the wrong ends. It is love for what harms. It is a disease of the soul and the heart that can infect the body as well. Ibn Taymiyya explains that the term "passionate love" is usually applied to a man's love for a woman or a young boy, to prohibited acts with women and boys, and to compulsive behavior toward wives, concubines, and children. He denounces anyone who promotes gazing at women or young boys or who engages in illicit sexual acts with them as a means of expressing love for God. The antidote for passionate love, according to Ibn Taymiyya, is pure love for God and fear of Him. As an example he cites the Prophet Joseph who was bought as a slave by the Egyptian named al-'Aziz. The wife of al-'Aziz was an idolater, and for this reason she could not resist passionate love getting the better of her. She lusted after Joseph and schemed to entrap him. Joseph, however, loved God fully and so did not suffer the torments of passionate love. He was able to resist the advances of al-'Aziz's wife. Love of God and fear of God cast out the destructive forces of passion.

Love, fear, and hope feature prominently in Sufi thinking on the stages of the spiritual path. Along with love, Ibn Taymiyya also speaks of fear and hope, not so much as stages on a spiritual path but as energies driving humanity toward God. The fundamental orientation is ethical, but emotion is not absent. A proper fear of God will frighten the believer away from sin and unbelief. A sincere love for God will grow into profound affection and attachment. True hope inspires perseverance through difficulty. The following passage is indicative of Ibn Taymiyya's reflection:

> Know that there are three things that move hearts toward God: love, fear and hope. The most powerful of them is love. It is sought and desired in itself because it is desired in [both] this world and the hereafter. This is different from fear, which fades away in the hereafter. God said, "Indeed, the friends of God will have no fear. They will not

> grieve" (Q. 10:62). The purpose of fear is to deter and to prevent deviation from the path. Love leads the servant on the way to his Beloved. His journey to Him depends on the degree of its weakness and strength. Fear prevents him from deviating from the path to the Beloved. Hope leads him on. (MF 1:95)

Elsewhere, Ibn Taymiyya observes that fear drives one away from God's torment. As with love, fear and hope should be directed to God alone. Fear of a creature or hope in a creature apart from God is another form of associating partners with God. Ultimately, love for God will find its fullest expression in keeping the law given to God's Prophet. In the Qur'an the Prophet was instructed to declare, "Say! 'If you love God, then follow me. God will love you and forgive you your sins'" (Q. 3:31).

DIVINITY AND LORDSHIP

As noted above, Ibn Taymiyya prioritizes worship and ethics over the more ontological concerns of Ash'ari theologians and some Sufis. He elaborates this priority in diverse ways. One way takes inspiration from the Fatiha, the short prayer at the beginning of the Qur'an. Ibn Taymiyya explains that the first half of the Fatiha invokes God's names, reminding us of God's character and praiseworthiness, while the second half calls on God for help and guidance. The fifth verse, "You alone we worship; you alone we ask for help" is the pivot between the two halves: "You alone we worship" brings the first half to an end, and "You alone we ask for help" begins the second half. The order is of utmost significance for Ibn Taymiyya. Worship is prior and all-embracing. Asking for help is part of worship in a certain way, but it has to do with what God does for humans, what God creates and provides. Humans easily forget to worship God, and they fail to address Him until they need help. The Fatiha counters this tendency by bringing worship of God to the fore. It is only within the context of worship that asking God for help finds its proper place.

Ibn Taymiyya expands on this by linking worship of God to God's "divinity" (*ilahiyya* or *uluhiyya*) and asking for help to God's "lordship" (*rabbaniyya* or *rububiyya*). "Divinity" here does not refer to God's transcendent being or unique creative power. To Ibn Taymiyya's mind, a god or divinity (*ilah*) is an object of worship and love. God (*Allah*) is the only object worthy of worship and love above all others. "Lordship" then refers to God's rule in the sense of God's power to create. The Lord (*Rabb*) is the sole creator and provider of everything in the world, human acts included. Here is one way in which Ibn Taymiyya expresses this: "Worship is linked to [God's] divinity. Because of this, the declaration of God's unity is 'There is no god but God'. This is not the same as someone who confesses His lordship and does not worship Him, or worships another god with Him. A god is that which the heart deifies with perfect love, exaltation, homage, honor, fear, hope, and the like" (MF 10:157).

Ibn Taymiyya then attaches the term *tawhid* – declaring God one – to divinity and lordship. He calls devoting worship solely to God *tawhid al-ilahiyya* and recognizing God as the sole creator *tawhid al-rububiyya*. The first is devoting all of life to God alone in worship. The second is intellectual assent to the fact that God is the origin of all things. Taking God as sole object of worship (*tawhid al-ilahiyya*) necessarily includes confessing God as sole lord and creator of the universe (*tawhid al-rububiyya*). The worshipper focused on God alone has no other sources of help in view.

Following on from this analysis, Ibn Taymiyya distinguishes two different kinds of *shirk*, that is, association of partners with God. *Shirk* in God's divinity is worshipping and loving creatures apart from God, as in the Qur'anic verse, "Some people take rivals apart from God. They love them with the love due to God. Those who believe are stronger in love for God" (Q. 2:165). *Shirk* in God's lordship is denying that He is the creator of everything that is and everything that takes place. Ibn Taymiyya believes that it is possible to affirm the exclusiveness of God's lordship while at the same time violating the claims of God's divinity. This was the state of the pre-Islamic polytheists who affirmed God as sole Creator while worshipping idols. This is the danger posed by Ash'ari theology inasmuch as it gives priority to God's lordship over God's divinity.

COMMAND AND CREATION

Ibn Taymiyya also seeks to ward off the perceived ontological excesses of Sufis and Ash'aris through analysis of the terms command (*amr*) and creation (*khalq*), and their many synonyms. God's command is typically synonymous with God's legislation, love, and good pleasure. God's creation is usually synonymous with God's determination, decree, and lordship, as well as God's ontological will, which is God's will that all created things should exist. There is a certain similarity between the term command and the term divinity (*ilahiyya*) inasmuch as both connote worship. However, divinity refers to God's worthiness to be an object of worship, whereas God's command refers to the specific worship and obedience that God requires of human beings.

Furthermore, Ibn Taymiyya observes that many Qur'anic terms appear sometimes in an ontological sense and at other times in a legislative sense, depending on their contexts. The term "will" (*irada*), for example, occurs in an ontological sense in the following Qur'anic passage: "Whomever God wills to guide, He opens his breast to Islam. Whomever He wills to misguide, He makes his breast narrow and tight as if he were climbing up to the sky" (Q. 6:125). Here God's will is determinative of what is. Human choice is not in view. However, the term "will" occurs in a legislative and religious sense in another verse: "God wills ease for you. He does not will difficulty for you" (Q. 2:185). God's "will" in this passage indicates that God loves and commands ease. It does not mean that God will always make life easy.

Ibn Taymiyya frequently deploys his distinction between legislation and ontology, between command and creation, to clarify disagreements with opponents. For example, as we saw in the previous chapter, the Sufi theorist Ibn al-'Arabi claims that the Children of Israel who worshipped the calf in the Sinai wilderness were actually worshipping God. He supports this by giving an ontological interpretation to the Qur'anic verse, "Your Lord has decreed that you worship none but Him" (Q. 17:23). For Ibn al-'Arabi all creatures are worshipping God in fact, no matter what their immediate objects of worship might be. Ibn Taymiyya counters that God's decree in this verse refers to God's command. God commands that no one should worship anyone but Him.

Ibn Taymiyya also clarifies his position by outlining three errors in command and creation. The first error is to emphasize command at the expense of creation. The culprits here are Muʿtazili theologians and those Twelver Shiʿis who follow them, like Ibn al-Mutahhar al-Hilli against whom Ibn Taymiyya wrote his massive *Way of the Sunna*. The Muʿtazilis insist that humans create their own acts in order to carve out an autonomous sphere for human action. If God created all human acts, including acts of disobedience, it would be unjust of God to punish those disobedient acts. Ibn Taymiyya rejects this because it posits multiple creators in the universe. It compromises God's exclusive creation of all things. While Ibn Taymiyya himself stresses ethics over ontology, he does not go so far as to deny God's creation of human acts. Humans commit their own acts and are responsible for them, but it is still God who creates them. I will discuss Ibn Taymiyya's understanding of the human act further in Chapter Eight.

The second error according to Ibn Taymiyya's outline is to emphasize God's creation, will, and determination of all things at the expense of God's command. He finds this in the Arab polytheists of the Qur'an who blame their polytheism on God's will (see Q. 6:148). They claim that they cannot help but worship idols because that is what God has determined. Ibn Taymiyya rejects this argument as irrational. Human society could not function if everyone was permitted to blame their crimes on God's will. God's will and determination of all things applies to everyone equally and is therefore not an argument for anyone. If someone violated someone else's wife or killed his son, the latter will not allow the former to excuse his action by blaming it on God's determination.

Worse than Arab polytheists, according to Ibn Taymiyya, are Sufi antinomians, that is, Sufis who think the law does not apply to them. The issue here is not merely excusing disobedience of God's command by resort to God's determination. It is that God's command falls away completely because humans disappear into the divine. Ibn Taymiyya identifies two ways in which this is said to happen. In the first, individual Sufis experience ecstatic union with God and conclude that the law no longer applies to them. An example is when Sufis in trance miss their prayers. Ibn Taymiyya counters that such Sufis are still living and willing beings who are accountable for their deeds. They are still subject to considerations of benefit and harm, which is what the law came to explicate.

Ibn Taymiyya finds a second kind of Sufi antinomianism among Ibn al-ʻArabi and his followers. Ibn Taymiyya accuses them of making God and the world identical and thereby abolishing any independent sphere of human moral agency subject to God's command and prohibition. However, things are not quite so simple, and Ibn Taymiyya recognizes this, at least sometimes. Ibn al-ʻArabi's theology is very difficult to pin down. He places ambiguity at the heart of reality, and there are always two ways of seeing things. From one perspective God is totally other and completely different from the existents of the universe. From the other perspective there is no Existent but God. Other existents only exist by virtue of receiving God's existence. Everything in existence is thus both God and not God.

Ibn Taymiyya appreciates the side of Ibn al-ʻArabi that distinguishes God and the world. Ibn al-ʻArabi is the closest of his kind to Islam. He upholds the law. He distinguishes between the God who manifests and the things manifested. Many people profit from his teaching, even if they do not perceive the pernicious reality of what he means. That reality, according to Ibn Taymiyya, is Ibn al-ʻArabi's other way of seeing things, which is that all existents are God. Ibn al-ʻArabi and his followers propagate the oneness of existence and the unification of God and creation. Their pantheism equates God with all sorts of filth in the world and erases all distinctions between good and evil. Ibn Taymiyya is especially disturbed by those who take this to extremes. He singles out the poet ʻAfif al-Din al-Tilimsani (d. 1291) as the most unbelieving of Ibn al-ʻArabi's followers. According to Ibn Taymiyya, al-Tilimsani fails to draw any distinction whatsoever between God and the world, and he explicitly affirms antinomianism. Ibn Taymiyya writes of the poet, "He used to make all forbidden things licit to the point that trustworthy witnesses even reported that he used to say, 'A girl, her mother, and a non-relative female are all the same. There is nothing forbidden to us in that'...and he used to say, 'The whole Qur'an is polytheism. There is no confession of God's oneness in it. Confession of God's oneness is in what we say'" (MF 2:472).

The third error according to Ibn Taymiyya's outline is to affirm both creation and command while impugning God's wisdom. Those who commit this error openly accuse God of foolishness and injustice in His actions in order to justify their unbelief. The main offender here is Iblis, the name of Satan in the Qur'an. God in the Qur'an commanded Iblis to bow down to the first man Adam, but Iblis refused, claiming that he was better than Adam. God then cast Iblis down to earth, and Iblis blamed God for misleading him. God commanded Iblis to prostrate but then created disobedience in him instead (Q. 7:11–18; 15:29–40). How could that be fair? In response to such dilemmas Ibn Taymiyya affirms the fundamental goodness in all that God does, no matter how apparently incomprehensible. God has a wise purpose in all that He creates and commands. In those cases where God commands one thing but creates another, it is for a wise purpose that God loves.

SAINTHOOD

Ibn Taymiyya elaborates the priority of worship and ethics over ontology through an analysis of sainthood. Ibn al-'Arabi is again a major opponent. He had many dreams and visions of spiritual realities that, according to his own understanding, penetrated to truths deeper than those found in the law of Muhammad and rationalist theology. While in his mid-thirties, Ibn al-'Arabi had a vision in Mecca confirming his status as the Supreme Seal of Muhammadan Sainthood. The Prophet Muhammad was surrounded by angels, the first four Sunni caliphs, and all of God's messengers with their communities. Jesus and Muhammad were talking, and then Muhammad asked Jesus to pull up a seat for Ibn al-'Arabi. The seat was designated for the heir of Muhammadan Sainthood. The implication is clear: Ibn al-'Arabi himself sits at the top of the spiritual hierarchy of the universe.

In Ibn al-'Arabi's theology, Muhammadan sainthood manifested a pre-existent Muhammadan Reality, which appeared in prophets and saints from Adam onward. The legislative side of this Reality was completed and sealed in the historical Muhammad, but the sainthood side continued until it was sealed in Ibn al-'Arabi. Even after that, the influence of former prophets continues on as the Great Universal Sainthood. Jesus will seal this Sainthood when he returns at the end of time. Then Jesus will come under the authority of the Seal of Muhammad Sainthood, and Ibn al-'Arabi will be the seal of all the saints. He will be the head of a spiritual elite privy to esoteric knowledge of ultimate reality.

Ibn Taymiyya rejects the notion that revelation of spiritual realities continues on beyond the legislative prophecy sealed in the Prophet Muhammad. Ibn al-'Arabi cannot be allowed to give priority to his private visions and mystical revelations over reason and the definitive and publicly accessible revelation of God to the Prophet. He might claim that his revelations came from the same source as the Prophet's revelation, but Ibn Taymiyya insists that prophetic revelation must be given priority over the products of mystical imagination.

In response to Ibn al-'Arabi's elitism and esotericism, Ibn Taymiyya recasts the notion of sainthood (*walaya*) in his characteristically ethical terms and replaces a hierarchy of esoteric knowledge with a hierarchy of obedience. What distinguishes God's saints or friends from God's enemies is not exclusive insight into reality or unique powers but belief in Muhammad and obedience to him. Saints properly divide into "the people on the right" and "those brought near to God" on the basis of performing the law (cf. Q. 56:8–11). "The people on the right" perform the obligatory works of the law, while "those brought near to God" perform further recommended deeds as well. True saints who happen to receive inspirations and visions subject them to the law to test their authenticity. Those who perform wonders do so only through the blessing that comes from following Muhammad. The best of people after Muhammad are the other prophets. The best of the saints are the first Sunni caliph Abu Bakr, then the subsequent three Sunni caliphs, and then the rest of the earliest Muslims (known as the Salaf). The saints are in no way superior to the prophets. Apart from the honored status of the prophets and the Salaf, Ibn Taymiyya's vision of sainthood is open to everyone who worships, loves, and obeys God alone by following His law. No one has privileged access to God on the basis of anything beyond that. The content of that law is the subject of the next chapter.

4

WORSHIP, LAW, AND INNOVATION

WORSHIP AND THE LAW

The previous chapter explored Ibn Taymiyya's two principles of worship – worship of God alone, and worship by means of God's law – and his distinctive concern for ethics in the face of challenges posed by Sufi and Ash'ari ontologies. This chapter expands on the second principle by taking a closer look at the content of worship. In the following text Ibn Taymiyya outlines what worship includes, which is much more than simply religious ritual.

> Worship is a term encompassing everything that God loves and is well pleased with, both words and deeds, both hidden and manifest. [It includes] ritual prayer, alms, fasting, pilgrimage [to Mecca], truthfulness in speech, discharging trusts, honoring parents, relating to relatives, fulfilling pledges, commanding the right and prohibiting the wrong, struggling against the unbelievers and hypocrites, beneficence to the neighbor, the orphan, the poor, the traveler, slaves, and animals, supplication, remembrance [of God], recitation [of the Qur'an], and such like. Likewise, love of God and His Messenger, fear of God and turning to Him, consecration of religion to Him, patience with His ruling, thanksgiving for His graces, good pleasure with His decree, complete trust in Him, hope in His mercy, fear of His chastisement, and such like. (MF 10:149–150)

Thus worship comprises everything that God loves. It embraces matters of ritual, social obligation, and spiritual virtue. It includes both what one says and what one does, both inwardly and outwardly. It involves the core rituals of Islam: the ritual prayer (*salah*), alms (*zakah*), fasting in the month of Ramadan, and the pilgrimage to Mecca (*hajj*). It includes other acts of religious devotion like supplication (*du'a*), remembrance of God (*dhikr*), and recitation of the Qur'an. It requires fulfilling obligations to members of one's family and society and taking responsibility for the quality of society's moral life by commanding the right and prohibiting the wrong and by struggling (*jihad*) against hypocrites and unbelievers. It also includes spiritual virtues like fear, thankfulness, hope, and love for God and His Messenger, the Prophet Muhammad. In mainstream Sunni thought, worship rituals and societal obligations are the concern of jurisprudence (*fiqh*) and spiritual virtues the concern of Sufism (*tasawwuf*). Ibn Taymiyya brings these two concerns together under the one rubric of worship.

Elsewhere Ibn Taymiyya identifies the content of worship with the law (*shari'a* and *shar'*). Law in the modern, secular sense is a system of rules for political, social, and economic interaction legislated by a state and backed up by state sanction. Ibn Taymiyya's understanding of law is theological and far more comprehensive. The foundation of the law is the Qur'an and the Sunna. The Sunna comprises the sayings and deeds of the Prophet Muhammad recorded in short reports called hadith. Furthermore, the law is best preserved, according to Ibn Taymiyya, in the teaching and practice of the Salaf, the earliest generations of Muslims following the Prophet. Later generations cannot attain the same degree of knowledge of the law because they are more distant in time from the revelatory events. Moreover, for Ibn Taymiyya the law encompasses both what one is to believe and what one is to do, both theological doctrines and the deeds of the body and the heart, both matters pertaining to religious ritual and affairs involving fellow human beings.

Ibn Taymiyya is well aware that his consolidation of both belief and action under the rubric of law is not the normal way to classify the religious sciences in his day. He notes that other scholars limit law to deeds only and that they study it in the realm of jurisprudence (*fiqh*).

Theological matters are then treated separately. Ibn Taymiyya rejects the limiting of law to deeds. For him the law includes both beliefs and deeds, both the inner and the outer. Law comprises everything discussed in Sufism, jurisprudence, and theology. Ibn Taymiyya is not without precedent in conceiving the law in this expansive and comprehensive fashion. It has roots in Hanbalism, and the Sufi theorist Ibn al-'Arabi views the law in much the same way. Ibn Taymiyya may have drawn inspiration on this point from Ibn al-'Arabi before turning against him in 1304.

Throughout his writings, Ibn Taymiyya is deeply concerned to clarify that not everything people think is law should be law, or at least not law for everyone. To this end, he distinguishes three kinds of law:

> The word "law" (*shar'*) in the custom of the people has taken on three meanings: the revealed law, the interpreted law, and the adulterated law. The revealed law (*al-shar' al-munazzal*) is the Book and the Sunna established by the Messenger. Following this law is obligatory for both the earlier and the later generations [of Muslims]. The best friends of God are the most perfect in following it. Whoever does not adhere to this law, whoever discredits it, or whoever permits anyone to deviate from it must be called upon to repent. Whoever does not repent is killed. The interpreted [law] (*mu'awwal*) is the rulings in which the scholars exercise independent reasoning (*ijtihad*). It is permissible to follow the authority of a founder (*imam*) among the founders [of the four Sunni law schools]. It is not obligatory for people to adhere to the view of a particular jurist. The adulterated law (*al-shar' al-mubaddal*) includes the fabricated hadiths, wrongheaded interpretations, and misguiding innovations that have been introduced into the law but do not belong to it. It is ruling by other than what God has revealed. It is not permitted for anyone to follow this and the like of it. (MF 11:506–507)

In this text Ibn Taymiyya first establishes the two primary sources of the revealed law: the Book, which is the Qur'an, and the Sunna of the Prophet. The revealed law is obligatory for everyone without exception. Ibn Taymiyya elsewhere equates the revealed law with justice (*'adl*): "The Book and justice are inseparable. The Book explicates the law. The law is justice, and justice is the law. Anyone who judges with justice judges with the law... The entire revealed law is justice" (MF 35:366). Ibn

Taymiyya's equation of the law with justice runs parallel to his equation of the law with benefit, which will be explained below, and his affirmation that revelation and reason agree, which will be noted in Chapter Seven. In each case, there is a perfect correlation between knowledge naturally accessible to human faculties and the revelation of God.

The second type of law, the interpreted law, is the domain of scholars and jurists who strive to ascertain the rulings of the law found in the revealed sources. This is the law of the four Sunni law schools. Ibn Taymiyya regards the independent reasoning (*ijtihad*) of these scholars as meritorious even when it produces incorrect results. He often quotes the saying of the Prophet, "If a judge exercises independent reasoning and is correct, he receives two rewards. If a judge exercises independent reasoning and errs, he receives one reward." For Ibn Taymiyya a correct ruling is one that agrees with the revealed law. It is rewarded twice by God. An incorrect ruling may be followed, but it may not be imposed on the whole community. It is rewarded once by God for the exertion of scholarly effort. The category of interpreted law affords Ibn Taymiyya space for generosity and liberality toward jurists with whom he disagrees. They may be wrong, but they are still worthy of respect and reward for their efforts. The scholarly search for the law is a good thing in itself.

Ibn Taymiyya's approach to the law is highly textualist. Every ruling of the revealed law and the interpreted law must be based on a text in the sources of revelation. The third type, the adulterated law, is everything that people imagine to be part of the law but in fact has no basis whatsoever in the revealed sources: "It is ruling by other than what God has revealed." Ibn Taymiyya does not permit following rulings with no foundation in the authentic texts of revelation.

Ibn Taymiyya devotes much of his scholarly effort to sifting what he believes to be adulterated law from revealed law and interpreted law. This chapter focuses especially on his concern to differentiate lawful worship rituals from those that he deems innovated (*bid'a*). The mainstream Sunni position at Ibn Taymiyya's time was that some innovated rituals were good. For example, it was argued that the second Sunni caliph 'Umar introduced a good innovation in the *tarawih* prayers. These are additional recommended prayers during the nights of the fasting month of Ramadan. Ibn Taymiyya takes the strict view that all innovations are unlawful on the grounds that the Prophet said, "Every innovation is an error." However, he does not reject *tarawih* prayers in particular. Instead, he explains that 'Umar only "innovated" them in a linguistic sense, not a legal sense, because in fact the prayers had precedents in the practice of the Prophet Muhammad himself. Ibn Taymiyya also permits doing something new after the death of the Prophet out of need, like collecting the Qur'an into one book, but this is again only an innovation linguistically, not legally. However, Ibn Taymiyya does identify many unacceptable innovations in the beliefs and practices of his time, and a number of these are linked to Sufism.

WORSHIP RITUALS: LAWFUL AND INNOVATED

Sufi spiritual disciplines and the Sufi cult of the saints had gained wide popularity and public prominence in Egypt and Syria by the end of the thirteenth century. One common Sufi devotional practice was the spiritual concert (*sama'*), which included playing musical instruments, clapping hands, and dancing to promote ecstatic mystical states. Ibn Taymiyya relates the following account of his own experience of a spiritual concert.

> In the early part of my life, I found myself with a group of the adherents of asceticism, worship and will [i.e. Sufis] who were among the best of this kind. We passed the night somewhere. They wanted to perform a spiritual concert, and they wanted me to participate with them. I refused to do that. So, they arranged a place for me off to the side, and I sat there. When they were performing their spiritual concert and ecstasy and mystical states overtook them, the grand shaykh called out to me in his ecstatic state. He said, "You over there! A great fortune has come to you! Come take your fortune!" I said to myself, and then to them openly when we had regathered, "You can have this fortune. I will not partake in any part of a fortune that does not come via the path of [the Prophet] Muhammad Ibn 'Abd Allah." It became clear to those among them with awareness and knowledge that others among them were satans and others drunk with wine. The meaning of what I said is that the cause of

> this "fortune" – this gift, this present, this mystical state – is not lawful. It is not an act of obedience to God and His Messenger. The Messenger did not legislate it. It is like someone saying, "Come drink wine with us, and we will give you this money," or, "Venerate this idol, and we will give you authority over this province," and such like. (MF 10:418–419)

This account shows that Ibn Taymiyya spent time with Sufis, at least early in his life. He was well acquainted with their practices. Perhaps he had even participated in such rituals before. Yet, on this occasion, he chose to withdraw, and he condemns this kind of spiritual concert as falling outside the law of God. The "fortune" offered by the grand shaykh came from dubious sources.

This anecdote appears near the end of Ibn Taymiyya's short treatise *Worship Rituals* (MF 10:387–421). The aim of the treatise is to distinguish worship rituals that are lawful (*mashru'*) from those that are innovated. Ibn Taymiyya envisions a rich spirituality within the realm of the lawful, including a lawful Sufism. Lawful rituals bring one near to God and are the path to God. They are acts of righteousness, obedience, and goodness. They are performed by those who follow the way of asceticism, poverty, and Sufism. Some lawful worship rituals are obligatory, like the five daily prayers, fasting in the month of Ramadan, giving alms, and travelling to Mecca for the pilgrimage. Other lawful rituals are recommended, like fasting three days a month and giving alms beyond what is obligatory. Ibn Taymiyya provides a long list of rituals that are lawful if performed in a lawful manner. These include night vigils, reciting the Qur'an, offering up supplications and invocations, traveling to Mecca and the mosques of Medina and Jerusalem, and various kinds of jihad.

The primary examples of unlawful rituals mentioned in *Worship Rituals* are innovated spiritual retreats (*khalwa*) and remembrance of God (*dhikr*), as well as spiritual concerts. Ibn Taymiyya complains that people go on spiritual retreat to graveyards and caves in the mountains. Such places are out of earshot of a prayer call and have no mosque in which to pray the five daily prayers. Graveyards are especially dangerous. People imagine that they see and talk with long-dead pious people and even prophets. Ibn Taymiyya says visions and dreams of the pious and the prophets are often in fact satanic impersonations.

Nevertheless, he does not entirely condemn spiritual retreats. It is permitted and even recommended to isolate oneself in a secluded place to study or to avoid forbidden and unprofitable activities. The Prophet and his Companions secluded themselves in mosques. However, one must not isolate oneself to the point of missing prayer in the congregation or failing to fulfill other duties.

Remembrance of God is the devotional exercise of repeating God's names. Ibn Taymiyya affirms the use of compound expressions like "Glory be to God," and "There is no god but God alone and without partner." However, he censures repetition of single names like "God, God" or "He, He" as innovations that are linguistically meaningless and irrational. He explains that some Sufis repeat these single word expressions to focus the heart and prepare the soul for mystical inrushes. Ibn Taymiyya sarcastically dismisses such inrushes as satanic states. Satan deceives the mystic into believing that he has attained an exalted state even higher than that of the Prophet Muhammad.

Ibn Taymiyya reserves his sharpest criticism in *Worship Rituals* for spiritual concerts of the kind that he witnessed in the anecdote above. He prefaces his remarks with a story about wine attributed to the third Sunni caliph ʿUthman Ibn ʿAffan. A man propositioned a woman for sex. She told him that he would first have to prostrate before an idol. He refused, saying he could not worship an idol alongside God. She said he would have to kill a boy. He refused to do that as well. So she invited him to drink a goblet of wine. He drank. Then he killed the boy, prostrated to the idol, and fornicated with the woman. Ibn Taymiyya extends the moral of this tale to spiritual concerts. The music of spiritual concerts is the wine of souls. Music leads to idolatry as devotees love their spiritual masters more than they love God. Music and singing lead the chaste down the road to moral perversity and even murder.

SPIRITUAL CONCERT AND ANNIHILATION

Ibn Taymiyya has little good to say in *Worship Rituals* about the term "spiritual concert". He is more discriminating in *Spiritual Concert and Dance* (MF 11:557–602), a compilation of his writings on spiritual concerts collected after his death. Ibn Taymiyya often appropriates a term used by his interlocutors and distinguishes their allegedly incorrect understandings from a correct understanding that accords with his own religious doctrine. For Ibn Taymiyya, the correct and lawful spiritual concert is listening to God's verses in the Qur'an, listening to the prophets, and listening to people of knowledge. The unlawful spiritual concert of the pre-Islamic polytheists and the Sufis is clapping, whistling, and listening to music. The musical instruments of the Sufis were not known among the Salaf, the earliest generations of Muslims. They are innovations. Ibn Taymiyya says that the Prophet did allow women to play the tambourine at weddings and to engage in other types of entertainment, but men did not do such things. It is in fact effeminate for men to sing. Ibn Taymiyya supports these views with many quotations from the Qur'an, reports of the Prophet's words and deeds called hadith, and the sayings of the Salaf.

Elsewhere in his corpus, Ibn Taymiyya appropriates the Sufi term "annihilation" (*fana'*) in a similar manner. Annihilation is typically understood to be the ecstatic experience of passing away in God in the course of spiritual concerts and devotional exercises. Ibn Taymiyya describes this state as so intense that it leads to absence from oneself and others and disappearance into the object of worship. He says that this experience is good insofar as the heart draws near to God, but defective inasmuch as one loses awareness of oneself. Such a state is excusable but not praiseworthy. It is better to keep a clear mind as the Prophet and his Companions did.

Ibn Taymiyya outlines three types of annihilation. The correct type is the annihilation of willing, worshipping, and loving anything other than God. This is the annihilation attained by the prophets and the saints. It is worshipping God lawfully, and it does not necessarily involve ecstatic experience. A person in this state, Ibn Taymiyya explains, fears God, hopes in Him, completely trusts Him, and loves Him to the exclusion of all other fears, hopes, trusts, and loves.

The second type is the annihilation of witnessing (*shuhud*) anything but God. Ibn Taymiyya says that this occurs to those who in their weakness of heart become so absorbed in remembrance of God that they fail to notice anything else. He censures those who imagine that they have become their Beloved and those who think that they are witnessing the secret of God's determination of all things and the rulings of God's lordship. Such people make annihilation the sole objective of their spiritual journey. They downgrade the importance of the law by failing to differentiate between God's command and God's prohibition. Ibn Taymiyya counters that correct witnessing is not about gaining union with God or insight into the secrets of reality. It is about confessing that God is Lord and Creator and obeying God and His messengers.

A third type is annihilation of the existence (*wujud*) of everything but God. Ibn Taymiyya elaborates: "It is to bear witness that nothing exists except God and that the existence of the Creator is the very existence of the creation, without distinction between the Lord and the servant" (MF 10:222). Ibn Taymiyya attributes this view to Ibn al-'Arabi and his followers. He rejects it outright as unbelief because it collapses the ontological distinction between Creator and creature. He argues that it is wrong to conclude from an ecstatic experience of feeling completely at one with God that nothing exists except God.

It is clear that Ibn Taymiyya does not entirely banish emotion and ecstasy from lawful religion. However, he is very wary of anything that clouds the mind and leads to incorrect belief, immorality, or idolatry. He believes that worshipping within the confines of the law is the correct path to God and leads to the greatest benefit.

BENEFIT AND THE LAW

The textual foundations of Ibn Taymiyya's religious views are the Qur'an and the Sunna of the Prophet. Parallel to this, he invokes considerations of benefit (*maslaha*). His treatise *Spiritual Concert and Dance* provides a clear example. At the beginning of the treatise, Ibn Taymiyya explains that the different types of spiritual concert should be judged by whether they bring profit in religion or whether they bring trouble. Later in the book, he notes that the spiritual concert that God commands brings the effects of faith. Clapping and listening to music, however, bring no profit or benefit. Engaging in correct spiritual concert is not just a matter of doing what God commands. It is also doing what is beneficial and profitable.

Ibn Taymiyya presents one of his most forthright statements on benefit and the law in his treatise *Miracles and Wonders* (MF 11:311–362). Among other things, this treatise addresses whether Sufi mystical inspirations and wonder-working are of any profit to religion. Ibn Taymiyya's response is that mystical inspirations and wonders only yield advantage if they also happen to be righteous deeds commanded by the law. Following the law will always be profitable. However, there is no guarantee that mystical inspirations and wonders bring any advantage, and they may be positively harmful. Certainly, he notes, there can be no profit in this life or the hereafter in the wonders of riding a lion when there is no need to do so or walking on water when it is possible to cross the water by a bridge. Moreover, in the key passage quoted below, Ibn Taymiyya goes on to make the apologetic assertion that the law is coextensive with human benefit. Maximum human benefit is found in adherence to the law, and there is no benefit outside the law. Those who think they have located a benefit outside the law are mistaken. Either such people do not realize that the benefit is found in the law, or the benefit is not a true benefit.

> The principle overall is that the law (*shari'a*) never neglects a benefit (*maslaha*). Indeed, God has perfected the religion for us and completed the blessing. The Prophet has indeed spoken about everything that will bring us closer to the Garden of Paradise... One of two possibilities must obtain for the rational person who believes that something is a benefit even though the revelation does not mention it. Either the revelation indicates it and the person looking into it does not know it. Or it is not a benefit even though he believes it to be a benefit. Benefit is profit that accrues and predominates. Often people imagine that something is profitable in religion and in this world, when in fact its profit is outweighed by harm. As [God] said about wine and gambling, "Say! In these two is a great sin and profits for the people. Their sin is greater than their profit" (Q. 2:219). (MF 11:344–345)

Ibn Taymiyya's view cuts across the notion of unstated benefit (*maslaha mursala*) advocated by the prominent Shafi'i jurist and theologian al-Ghazali (d. 1111). For al-Ghazali the revealed law of Islam does not indicate every act that is beneficial. Some benefits are unstated and unattested. An unstated benefit may be identified and used as a justification for a new ruling. However, identifying legally relevant benefits can be highly subjective. So al-Ghazali developed a framework to guide the process. He examined the revealed law and inferred that its purposes consisted in the preservation of five things: religion, intellect, life, progeny, and property. The purpose of preserving intellect, for example, derives from the Qur'an's prohibition of wine because it intoxicates. An unstated benefit must correspond to one of the purposes of the law in order to support a new ruling.

Ibn Taymiyya rejects al-Ghazali's five-purposes-of-the-law scheme for two reasons. First, it adds to the revealed law by legislating rulings that God did not legislate. It adds rulings to the law through so-called unstated benefits that are not in fact beneficial. Second, the scheme of five purposes is too narrowly focused on the concerns of this world. It fails to consider the full breadth of benefits spoken to by the law, especially the benefits of worship rituals. It thus leads to neglect of obligatory and recommended deeds. Ibn Taymiyya maintains that the law deals comprehensively with benefit. It does not leave any part of human life out, and maximum utility is found in following the law in its entirety. Conversely, acts that lie outside the law are detrimental and harmful.

INNOVATED FESTIVALS AND THE PROPHET'S BIRTHDAY

Ibn Taymiyya critiques innovated rituals on the basis of both revelation and benefit in his large book *The Necessity of the Straight Path* (*Iqtida' al-sirat al-mustaqim*). The main objective of this book is to warn Muslims against participating in innovated festivals and imitating non-Muslims in their dress and behavior. Ibn Taymiyya does not require complete segregation of Muslims from non-Muslims. However, he does believe that Muslims spending too much time with non-Muslims and similarity in clothing and appearance lead to unacceptable friendship and mutual affection across the religious divide. So he stipulates, for example, that

Muslim men should dye their beards so as to differ from Jews and Christians, who do not dye their beards. Differing in outward behavior prevents going astray and clearly distinguishes the rightly guided from those who err. Ibn Taymiyya grounds all of this in the Qur'an, the Sunna of the Prophet, the Salaf, and early traditions such as the Pact of 'Umar, which stipulates how non-Muslims are to dress and conduct themselves while living under Muslim rule.

Similarly, Ibn Taymiyya asserts that sharing in non-Muslim religious rituals and festivals leads eventually to similarity in character and belief. He says that this is a problem especially among women. Muslims should not celebrate Palm Sunday and Maundy Thursday, paint Easter eggs, or participate in the Christian cult of Mary. Otherwise they will start to think that all religions worship the same God and differ only in worship practices. They will become more and more like Christians and even get baptized. Muslims should also differ from Jews and Christians by not turning graves into places of worship. Otherwise people might draw images of the deceased on the walls of the graves, worship those images, and end up in idolatry.

Parallel to his critique from the revealed sources in *The Necessity of the Straight Path*, Ibn Taymiyya weighs up considerations of benefit and detriment (*mafsada*). Innovations in festivals and other rituals may involve some measure of profit. Jews and Christians may derive some advantage from performing their own rites. However, all of this benefit is outweighed by the greater evil in those activities. If the good in non-Muslim practices did outstrip their evil, the law would have commanded them from the outset. The prescriptions of Islam coincide fully with what is beneficial to humanity, and anything else can only detract from this. Muslims, Ibn Taymiyya argues, will therefore derive benefit by intentionally differing from non-Muslims.

Ibn Taymiyya also critiques innovated Muslim festivals in *The Necessity of the Straight Path*. One example is the festival of the Prophet's Birthday (*mawlid al-nabi*), which Muslims in Ibn Taymiyya's time celebrated on a wide scale. It was commonly regarded as a good innovation, although some scholars rejected it as unlawful and worthless. Ibn Taymiyya takes a subtler approach. He does reject celebration of the Prophet's Birthday as unlawful because it has no support in the Qur'an and the Sunna and explains that Christians established festivals to commemorate events in the life of Jesus, but Muslims do not turn events in the life of their Prophet into festival days. The only Islamic festivals are those that God and the Prophet Muhammad have legislated. Nevertheless, Ibn Taymiyya recognizes different intentions among those who celebrate the Prophet's Birthday. He condemns those who celebrate it simply to imitate Christians who celebrate Christmas, but he allows that some celebrate it out of great love for the Prophet. The latter may receive a "great reward" (*ajr 'azim*) for their worthy intention and their exercise of independent legal reasoning in finding the ritual lawful, even if there is no reward in practicing the innovated festival itself. While the only proper way to show love for the Prophet is to follow his Sunna, Ibn Taymiyya is alert to the fact that people do not give something up without replacing it with something else. So he cautions against calling people away from celebration of the Prophet's Birthday unless they can be guided to replace it with something lawful and better, not something even worse.

Ibn Taymiyya's approach to the Prophet's Birthday and non-Muslim rituals is similar to his attitude toward the Sufi ecstatic experience of annihilation (*fana'*). He allows that annihilation may bring someone closer to God, even if not in the best fashion, and in much the same way he recognizes the possibility of good intention and benefit in celebration of the Prophet's Birthday, even if it remains unlawful and detrimental overall. Non-Muslims may likewise derive some benefit from their rituals but not enough to overcome their detriment. For Ibn Taymiyya, the law is the repository of full benefit. Yet his careful attention to intention and benefit enables him to take a nuanced view of the spiritual value of worship practices lying outside the scope of the law.

Polemically-minded modern-day Sufis and Salafis have taken this in different directions. Some Sufis have pounced on Ibn Taymiyya's statement that those who celebrate the Prophet's Birthday will receive a "great reward" in order to claim that he approves of the festival. Salafis focus on Ibn Taymiyya's criticism of the Prophet's Birthday and generally ignore the "great reward" remark or dismiss its significance. It does not fit easily with their view of Ibn Taymiyya as defender of the law against innovation.

GRAVE VISITATION AND INTERCESSION

Ibn Taymiyya is also greatly concerned about innovations surrounding the visitation of graves (*ziyarat al-qubur*). He treats the relevant issues in *The Necessity of the Straight Path* and many other texts. Ibn Taymiyya was well acquainted with shrine culture and probably even participated in it in early life. He writes, "I and others used to follow the doctrine of the fathers in [visiting graves]... We used to uphold the views of the innovators. When it became clear to us what the Messenger had brought, we had to decide whether to follow what God had revealed or to follow what we had found our fathers doing. It was obligatory to follow the Messenger" (MF 6:258). Across his works, Ibn Taymiyya speaks of oaths, vows, supplications, animal sacrifices, and the names of graves that pilgrims visited. He says that God honors and shows mercy to the saints and the righteous among the dead and amazing wonders occur at their graves. Their graves are protected from animals, fire, and evil spirits, and it is advantageous to be buried near them. He also maintains that visiting graves is lawful and that it can be beneficial. Lawful grave visitation includes greeting the dead, supplicating for them, and visiting them in order to remind oneself of one's mortality.

Despite all this, Ibn Taymiyya is most profoundly worried that shrine religion will descend into idolatry and polytheism (*shirk*). The crux of the issue is supplication (*du'a*) and intercession (*shafa'a*). Saints and their graves were regarded as repositories of blessing and, according to Ibn Taymiyya, people too readily turned to the dead in their time of need instead of to God. He forbids supplicating a dead saint or prophet directly because it is outright polytheism. He also prohibits asking a saint or prophet to intercede before God. He does acknowledge that the Companions sought the Prophet Muhammad's intercession while he was still alive. However, this does not give license for seeking intercession from the Prophet at his grave. The proper way to seek access to God through the Prophet is to believe in him and obey him.

Ibn Taymiyya explains that it is unbelief and polytheism to think that intermediaries are required to access God in the same way that intermediaries are required to access a king. Unlike a king, God knows the affairs of His creatures directly and needs no help in dealing with them. God also needs no prodding to treat His creatures well. Therefore, Ibn Taymiyya argues, only God can be asked to forgive sins and guide hearts. The only intercession that is acceptable to God is that which God Himself permits, such as His permission to the Prophet Muhammad, other prophets, and other righteous persons to intercede before God in the hereafter, especially for believers whose sins earn them a temporary place in Hell-Fire. Ibn Taymiyya also criticizes praying directly to God in the name of a saint or prophet, even if this is not as bad as praying directly to a living saint or asking a dead saint to intercede. Furthermore, he argues that performing the ritual prayer at graves and turning graves into mosques have been prohibited in order to avert the temptations of idolatry. These things would have been permitted had their benefit outweighed their harm. Instead, domes and mosques built over graves must be demolished. So far as we know, Ibn Taymiyya himself did not destroy any funerary monuments, but his sentiments have inspired such iconoclastic acts by Wahhabis and modern jihadis.

As noted above, Ibn Taymiyya does permit visiting graves to greet the dead, offer supplications for them, and benefit from the reminder of one's mortality. Nevertheless, he attempts to undercut shrine religion by denouncing travel for the sole intention of visiting graves, even for the purpose of visiting the Prophet's grave in Medina. Ibn Taymiyya grounds his position in the Prophet's statement, "Do not undertake travel except to three mosques," namely, the mosques of Mecca, Medina, and Jerusalem. Travelling to graves deliberately to perform supplications is disliked because it resembles the practices of pre-Islamic times. It distracts from legislated rituals like the pilgrimage to Mecca, and it diverts from worshipping God alone.

Ibn Taymiyya also seeks to undermine the shrine cults by denying that a place can be inherently sacred. He deems the virtue of a place to be a function of the moral virtue of the people living in it, not of the place itself. Ibn Taymiyya says that God has designated some places to be especially efficacious, such as the mosques in Mecca, Medina, and Jerusalem, but that is by virtue of God's designation. Places are not holy in and of themselves. In this light, supplication at graves is no more efficacious than supplication anywhere else. Even asking God to help the dead, which Ibn Taymiyya permits, is no more effective at their graves than elsewhere.

Many other aspects of shrine religion receive Ibn Taymiyya's censure. He criticizes making vows to dead saints and offering animal sacrifices at graves. He condemns kissing the ground in front of a grave, touching and kissing graves, lighting candles over graves at night, leaving supplications on notes at graves, sprinkling graves with rose water and perfume, and making a living as a grave custodian. He also complains that grave cults had led to the spread of many lies. Graves had been identified incorrectly, and fanciful legends had grown up around the shrines.

Ibn Taymiyya's arguments did not dampen enthusiasm for shrine religion in the Mamluk Empire. As we saw at the end of Chapter Two, opposition to his views on grave visitation led to his final demise. After Ibn Taymiyya died, the Shafi'i jurist Taqi al-Din al-Subki wrote a refutation that affirmed travel to Medina solely for the purpose of visiting the Prophet's grave. Al-Subki supports his case with the hadith reporting the Prophet's statement, "My intercession (*shafa'a*) is guaranteed for whoever visits my grave." Ibn Taymiyya considered this hadith report weak in its authenticity or simply forged. Al-Subki also charges Ibn Taymiyya with exaggerating the abuses surrounding grave visitation. It does not necessarily lead to polytheism, and it is not in fact an innovation because there are precedents from the time of the Prophet.

IBN TAYMIYYA AND SUFISM

By now it is clear that Ibn Taymiyya worked out his vision of worship in dialogue with Sufism and shrine religion. What then was his relationship to Sufism? This question has been much discussed in modern scholarship. Ibn Taymiyya's criticism of Ibn al-'Arabi and practices like spiritual concert and remembrance of God has earned him a reputation in many quarters as an implacable foe of Sufis. Yet others have called Ibn Taymiyya a "neo-Sufi" for emphasizing the original moral impulse of Sufism. The American scholar George Makdisi (d. 2002) even claimed to have found evidence that Ibn Taymiyya was himself a Sufi of the Qadiriyya order.

As observed in this and the previous chapter, Ibn Taymiyya's spirituality is distinctively ethical in character. The goal of the spiritual path is not ecstatic or metaphysical union with God, but perfect obedience to God's law found in the Qur'an and the Sunna. Lawful worship – including both ritual acts and spiritual dispositions of the heart – is the means by which human beings draw close to God. Based on these criteria, Ibn Taymiyya sifts what he considers to be correct in historical Sufism from what he believes to be innovation and unbelief.

Furthermore, Ibn Taymiyya translates the spirituality that he deems faithful to the law into the Sufi terminology of his day. He fills Sufi terms like spiritual concert (*sama'*), remembrance of God (*dhikr*), annihilation (*fana'*), and sainthood (*walaya*) with the content of his moral vision. He writes warmly of love, fear, and hope to give this vision a spiritual tone, and this is why his spirituality is sometimes called neo-Sufism.

George Makdisi labels Ibn Taymiyya a Sufi of the Qadiriyya order on the basis of a spiritual initiation chain that he found linking him back to the Hanbali 'Abd al-Qadir al-Jilani (d. 1166), the eponym of the Qadiriyya order. Makdisi also found two statements in which Ibn Taymiyya says that he donned the Sufi cloak of 'Abd al-Qadir. "Donning the cloak" is an initiation ritual into a Sufi chain of spiritual authority. Ibn Taymiyya calls 'Abd al-Qadir "our shaykh" in his commentary on parts of 'Abd al-Qadir's *Openings of the Unseen* (MF 10:455–548). Makdisi also cites the fact that Ibn Taymiyya was buried in a Sufi cemetery.

Others have cast doubt on Makdisi's evidence. Initiation chains are often forged. The two statements about donning the Sufi cloak appear in texts written by other scholars after Ibn Taymiyya's death, and they could also have been forged. Ibn Taymiyya criticizes the Sufi initiation ritual of donning the Sufi cloak in his own writings, and no evidence has been found in his works that he participated in such a ritual himself. As for the commentary, Ibn Taymiyya does show much appreciation for 'Abd al-Qadir's moral insights and calls him "our shaykh," but the work does not provide any further evidence that Ibn Taymiyya belonged to a Sufi order. Moreover, the Qadiriyya Sufi order was still in the process of formation in Ibn Taymiyya's time. So it is not clear that there yet existed a well-formed Qadiriyya order to join. It only gained its widespread popularity later on. Finally, Ibn Taymiyya did not call himself a Sufi, and the significance of being buried in a Sufi cemetery is uncertain.

Despite the ambiguous nature of the evidence, it remains possible that Ibn Taymiyya participated in organized Sufism in his early years. The spiritual concert anecdote translated earlier in this chapter shows that he did associate with Sufis at some point, even if he refused to participate in their spiritual concert on that occasion. He may have joined in with spiritual concerts before that, but it is highly unlikely that he participated in organized Sufi activities in his later years. If Ibn Taymiyya is to be called a Sufi, it must be strictly on his own terms of a highly ethicized spirituality.

A more illuminating approach to the question is Ibn Taymiyya's legal assessment of Sufism. In a short treatise on Sufi origins (MF 11:5–24), he says that the term "Sufi" became well-known only after the first three Islamic centuries. Sufis first appeared in the Iraqi city of Basra, which was known for extremes in asceticism and piety. There was even a story of people swooning and dying from listening to the Qur'an. Ibn Taymiyya explains that the Basrans, out of their intense experiences, exercised independent reasoning (*ijtihad*) to derive rulings concerning worship, just as their neighbors in Kufa exercised independent reasoning in matters of governance. Certain Basran rulings deviated from the guidance of the Qur'an, the Prophet, and the Salaf, and this led to controversy. Some criticized the Sufis as innovators while others praised them as the best of people after the prophets. Ibn Taymiyya commends a more discriminating assessment. Sufi independent reasoning based on intuited inspiration (*ilham*) may at times be superior to weak methods used by some jurists. Independent reasoning brings some Sufis closer to God, while it leads others into error and disobedience. Some became innovators, like al-Hallaj (d. 922) who was crucified for heresy. Other Sufis such as al-Junayd (d. 910) and 'Abd al-Qadir al-Jilani stayed within the bounds of the law.

For Ibn Taymiyya Sufism is ultimately the product of meritorious independent legal reasoning. It is correct as long as it stays within the limits of the revealed law. Yet Sufi independent reasoning sometimes produces errors, innovations, and unbelief. In terms of Ibn Taymiyya's typology of revealed, interpreted, and adulterated law outlined earlier in this chapter, Sufism falls under the category of interpreted law, with some of it coming under adulterated law. In the end, however, it does not matter to Ibn Taymiyya what Sufism is or is not. What matters to him is a spirituality in conformity to the revealed law. The next chapter takes a closer look at how he himself derives that law.

5

JURISTIC AUTHORITY AND DERIVING GOD'S LAW

THE SUNNI LAW SCHOOL SYSTEM

The previous chapter noted that Ibn Taymiyya views Sufism as a product of independent reasoning. He regards the four Sunni law schools in the same way. He locates the Hanafi, Maliki, Shafi'i, and Hanbali law schools within his category of interpreted law, lying between the revealed law and the adulterated law. Yet Ibn Taymiyya worries that the Sunni law school system of his time had acquired some of the authority that he reserves for the revealed law, and he seeks to put the law schools back in their place.

The main sources of law in Sunni legal reasoning are the Qur'an, the Sunna (the sayings and deeds of the Prophet recorded in hadith reports), consensus, and analogy. The Qur'an and the Sunna are textual sources. Those who exercise independent reasoning (*ijtihad*) and derive the law directly from these texts are called absolute *mujtahid*s. The term *mujtahid* is derived from the same Arabic root as *ijtihad*, and it refers to someone who engages in independent reasoning. Famous absolute *mujtahid*s include the eponyms of the four Sunni law schools: Abu Hanifa (d. 767), Malik Ibn Anas (d. 796), al-Shafi'i (d. 820), and Ahmad Ibn Hanbal (d. 855).

Consensus (*ijma'*), the third source of the law, functions like a text. Full agreement of the jurists or the Muslim community in any era on a ruling ends all future discussion of the issue, and the ruling becomes part of the law. As noted in Chapter Two, Taqi al-Din al-Subki accused Ibn Taymiyya of breaching consensus on divorce oaths. Ibn Taymiyya argued that violation of a divorce oath did not result in an actual divorce. Al-Subki replied that a divorce does occur, and he grounded this in consensus:

> When the Community has come to consensus that a divorce occurs, no one is permitted to oppose [the Community], for consensus is among the strongest of legal proofs. God has protected this Community from coming to consensus on an error. Its consensus is correct. Many of the scholars express the view that one who opposes the consensus of the Community is an unbeliever. (*Durra* 14)

The primary tool of *mujtahids* is analogy (*qiyas*), the fourth source of the law. The classic case of analogy is the prohibition of date wine by comparison to grape wine (*khamr*), which the Qur'an forbids (Q. 5:90). The jurists discerned that grape wine was forbidden because it intoxicates. Date wine also intoxicates, and therefore it was forbidden as well.

As Sunni jurists settled into legal schools in the medieval period, reasoning directly from the Qur'an and the Sunna fell into disuse. For the most part jurists conformed to the legal doctrines of their respective schools, and they addressed legal questions by citing their schools' precedents. If they did not find exact precedents, they exercised independent reasoning as affiliated *mujtahids* by interpreting the school's precedent literature much as absolute *mujtahids* had earlier interpreted the Qur'an and the Sunna. Jurists within schools also developed additional principles for adapting to new circumstances. The Shafi'i jurist al-Ghazali, for example, derived new rules on the basis of benefit (*maslaha*) within a framework of five purposes of the law: preservation of religion, intellect, life, progeny, and property. This was noted in the previous chapter. Overall, legal development took place within the wider context of legal conformism (*taqlid*) to the schools. Hanafis worked within the Hanafi law school, Shafi'is within the Shafi'i school, and so on.

This system of following authorities who mediate between the original sources of the religion and later generations of jurists provided stability in the midst of diversity. The four schools recognized each other as equally acceptable expressions of Sunni Islam based on the Qur'an and the Sunna of the Prophet. They maintained stability by limiting direct reconsideration of what the Qur'an and the Sunna meant for the law. The consensus around this system also demarcated Sunnis from Shi'is by disallowing appeal to the authority of Shi'i *imams*. For Twelver and Isma'ili Shi'is, the *imams*, as descendants of the Prophet Muhammad appointed by God to lead the Muslim community, possessed definitive authority that Sunnis could not accept. Apart from that, the four Sunni schools differed and competed among themselves. Individual jurists, however, did not easily branch outside their own law schools, whether to adopt the view of another school or to follow an opposing text from the Qur'an or the Sunna of the Prophet. Breaking with the system risked error, unbelief, and chaos.

BACK TO THE QUR'AN AND THE SUNNA

Ibn Taymiyya adheres to the Sunni framework of rooting religious authority in the Qur'an, the Sunna, consensus, and analogy. However, he reconfigures it to assert the primacy of the Qur'an and the Sunna over against the prevailing system of legal conformism. Jurists of the four law schools sometimes followed rulings based on an analogy or a consensus that contradicted specific texts in the Qur'an or the Sunna in order to balance diverse legal considerations. Ibn Taymiyya counters that a correct analogy and a true consensus will never contradict a text from the Qur'an and the Sunna. If someone deploys an analogy that contradicts a text, it is not a valid analogy. Similarly, consensus cannot establish new law. It simply clarifies the Prophet's message, and it will never contradict the Qur'an and the Sunna. These assertions are part of Ibn Taymiyya's wider apologetic project. He maintains with firm conviction that the products of sound human reasoning will always agree with the revealed sources. Correct independent reasoning will never oppose a text, just as benefit and the law are coextensive and the human natural constitution (*fitra*) corresponds to the religion of Islam.

Additionally, Ibn Taymiyya strictly limits the scope of consensus. This turns the authority structure of the Sunni law schools on its head. According to Ibn Taymiyya, the only authoritative consensus is a consensus of the Companions of the Prophet or, less stringently, a consensus of the people of Medina up to the assassination of the third caliph 'Uthman Ibn 'Affan (d. 656). Ibn Taymiyya maintains that the Companions knew the Prophet's practice better than later generations and that the people of the Prophet's home city Medina preserved it best. If the Companions, who knew the Prophet best, differed over a matter, no later generation could erase those differing voices and come to a consensus, apart from an authentic text. Any alleged consensus of the eponyms of the four law schools or any other group of later scholars is not a proof. Legal doctrines that jurists claim were settled by a post-Companion consensus are in fact open to critique and correction.

Ibn Taymiyya does not reject legal conformism (*taqlid*) completely. No one can be an expert on every aspect of the law. A scholar may be a *mujtahid* in one area but not in another. Yet jurists should exercise independent reasoning from the Qur'an and the Sunna as much as possible. There is no reason, Ibn Taymiyya explains, to follow one law school submissively without question. The four school eponyms themselves commanded people not to conform unthinkingly to their rulings. The views of the school founders are not proofs. They could be wrong.

Ibn Taymiyya strips Sunni legal conformism of any pretension it might have to definitive religious authority. It no longer speaks for Islam as a whole. Yet he still seeks to show respect to his fellow jurists within the system. He wrote his treatise *Removal of Blame from the Great Imams* (MF 20:231–290) to explain how disputes arose among jurists and to clear the law school founders (the *imams*) of culpability when they oppose a hadith reporting the Prophet's Sunna. He begins *Removal of Blame* by establishing the sincerity of the founders and other jurists – none of them would intentionally oppose the Sunna of the Prophet. What then causes them to disagree? More specifically, why might they rule in opposition to an authentic hadith report? Ibn Taymiyya answers that the jurist may not know about the hadith or may have forgotten it.

It is not possible for any single jurist to know all of the hadith, not even a Companion of the Prophet. Later compilations of hadith may not be considered comprehensive, and it is not required to know all of the hadith literature to undertake independent reasoning. Additionally, a jurist might think that an authentic hadith report is not authentic because of some defect in the way the hadith reached him or because of disagreement among jurists over its authenticity. He may not fully understand the meaning of the hadith, or he may think the hadith is opposed by other evidence.

Going on in *Removal of Blame*, Ibn Taymiyya explains that different juristic apprehensions of the evidence lead to opposing views and conflicts. Each jurist is rewarded once for his effort and twice if he is correct. Sincerity should be assumed unless a jurist knowingly opposes authentic evidence. Even then, the jurist should be given the benefit of the doubt. However, the authentic hadith should be followed, not the jurist. Ibn Taymiyya elaborates:

> With respect to many hadiths, it is possible that the scholar has an argument for not acting on the hadith that we do not know about. The paths to knowledge are many, and we do not know everything that is in the hearts of the scholars. The scholar may disclose his argument, or he may not. If he has disclosed it, it may have reached us, or it may not have. If it has reached us, we may understand the point of his argument, or we may not, whether or not his argument is actually correct. However, even if we allow for all that, we are not permitted to turn away from a view whose argument is established by an authentic hadith and supported by a group of scholars and [turn] to a different view of another scholar who might know of something that opposes this argument, even if he is more knowledgeable. This is because the views of the scholars are more prone to error than are legal proofs. Legal proofs are the argument of God against all of His servants, unlike an opinion of a scholar. A legal proof cannot be in error if no other proof opposes it. This is not the case with the opinion of a scholar... The scholar might have an excuse for omitting [the legal proof], and we are excused for omitting his omission. (MF 20:250–251)

Ibn Taymiyya's plea for tolerance toward the great founders of the law schools, as well as scholars and jurists more generally, serves his own purposes. His plea envisions a world in which all jurists, and indeed all Muslims, are, like himself, subject only to the authority of the revealed texts and not to the views of other jurists or schools. It is a world in which individuals stand before God's revelation, or at least as much of it as has reached them, in intellectual freedom to discern the universal rulings of God's law to the best of their abilities. Sunni jurists had sacrificed some of that freedom for the sake of order and stability in the legal system. That is a sacrifice that Ibn Taymiyya does not always tolerate. Al-Dhahabi insightfully captures the dialectic of tolerance and intolerance in Ibn Taymiyya's approach:

> His manner is very much forgiving towards people, and he does not charge anyone with unbelief, unless he has presented a legal proof and an argument against him. Then he says, "This teaching is unbelief and misguidance. Its proponent is an ignorant independent reasoner (*mujtahid*) who has never been presented with the argument of God. Perhaps he will retract it or turn to God in repentance." (*Nubdha* 337)

The following discussions of Ibn Taymiyya's rulings on chess and triple divorce exemplify his legal methodology. The first case illustrates his use of analogy, and the second shows how he undermines an alleged consensus. In both cases he speaks as an absolute *mujtahid* assessing the evidence of the Qur'an and the Sunna independently of explicit affiliation with a law school. In the first case, his view happens to align with the traditional Hanbali ruling. In the second case, his ruling is at odds with all four Sunni law schools.

FORBIDDING CHESS

Chess was popular within the Mamluk Empire. Even some religious scholars played it. The dominant Shafi'is did not forbid it absolutely but ruled that the game was merely disliked or permitted. They only stipulated that chess should not be played in public and not for stakes, and that the players conduct themselves properly and not miss prayers. Ibn Taymiyya was once asked whether playing chess was forbidden, disliked, or permitted. He was also asked for the proof of his view. If he had been content to make his case as a Hanbali jurist, he could simply have cited the prevailing Hanbali opinion that chess is forbidden completely, even when not played for stakes, and then given a brief outline of the rationale for the ruling. Ibn Taymiyya aspired to more. In his fatwa responding to the inquiry (MF 32:216-239), he positions himself as an absolute *mujtahid* speaking independently of the four law schools. He is not merely working out the position of the followers of Ahmad Ibn Hanbal.

That said, Ibn Taymiyya still seeks to rally the law schools to his side by downplaying opposing views among the school eponyms. He reports that Abu Hanifa and Ahmad Ibn Hanbal forbade chess, even when played without stakes. He fudges the position of al-Shafi'i, saying that al-Shafi'i's dislike of chess is tantamount to prohibition. He does not mention reports that al-Shafi'i himself played chess. He also interprets Malik Ibn Anas's dislike of chess to mean prohibition. He does not inform his readers that some Maliki jurists allowed playing an occasional game of chess in the home.

Ibn Taymiyya cannot forbid chess simply by citing a text, as there are no texts in the Qur'an and the Sunna referring explicitly to chess. He also cannot appeal to a consensus of the Companions against chess because there are reports that some Companions played the game. Ibn Taymiyya does not tell his readers about these reports. He instead notes that the Companion 'Ali Ibn Abi Talib one day passed by some people playing chess and criticized them saying, "What are those statues that you are obsessed with?" He also observes that the Companion Ibn 'Umar prohibited chess, as did other Companions whom he does not name. Ibn Taymiyya does openly admit that some members of the early Muslim community after the Companions permitted chess without stakes, but he notes that one of them, a certain al-Sha'bi, only played it to avoid a greater evil. Al-Sha'bi was a Successor, a member of the generation after the Companions, and he played chess to soil himself morally and thereby disqualify himself from serving as a judge under the oppressive Umayyad governor al-Hajjaj Ibn Yusuf (d. 714).

With no explicit text from the Qur'an or the Sunna and no consensus of the Companions to decide the matter, Ibn Taymiyya forbids chess much as his Hanbali predecessors had done, by analogy to backgammon and gambling. Backgammon is not mentioned in the Qur'an, but the hadith literature censures it. The Prophet is reported to have said, "Whoever plays backgammon disobeys God and His Messenger," and, "Whoever plays backgammon is like someone who dips his hand into the flesh and blood of a pig." Most scholars across the four Sunni legal schools forbade backgammon on the basis of these statements, whether or not it was played for stakes. Ibn Taymiyya forbids it as well. He furthermore reports that Ahmad Ibn Hanbal and al-Shafi'i said that backgammon was worse than chess, while Malik Ibn Anas said that chess was worse. Ibn Taymiyya sides with Malik. He explains that Ahmad and al-Shafi'i only said backgammon was worse because they assumed it was played for stakes whereas chess was not.

Ibn Taymiyya explains that chess is worse than backgammon because it is highly addictive. It distracts hearts and minds from prayer and remembrance of God more than backgammon does, and even more than some kinds of wine and hashish. Ibn Taymiyya may be basing his judgement on direct observation. Al-Safadi, author of a major fourteenth-century biographical dictionary, underscores the chess obsession of a certain Nur al-Din who was an avid follower of Ibn Taymiyya's teaching. According to al-Safadi, Nur al-Din played chess day and night. He only ate or drank if he could not find someone to play against.

Ibn Taymiyya also forbids chess by analogy to the Qur'anic prohibition of *maysir*. *Maysir* was a pre-Islamic game played with arrows for the parts of a slaughtered animal. The Islamic tradition took the prohibition to apply to all forms of gambling. The Qur'an forbids *maysir* along with wine in the following verses: "O you who believe! Wine, *maysir*, idols, and divining arrows are filth of Satan's doing. So avoid it so that you might succeed. Satan only wants to incite enmity and hatred among you with wine and *maysir* and to distract you from remembrance of God and from prayer" (Q. 5:90–91). It is not immediately obvious that this text applies to chess. Ibn Taymiyya says that Shafi'is think *maysir* is forbidden only because it involves gambling and squandering wealth. As playing chess without stakes does not involve gambling, the prohibition of *maysir* does not apply and chess is not forbidden. Ibn Taymiyya disagrees. He reasons as follows. Even if *maysir* were forbidden merely because it squanders wealth, games like backgammon and chess would still be forbidden because they so easily lead to gambling. Games excite desire and readily degenerate into playing for stakes. Ibn Taymiyya here invokes a common Maliki and Hanbali juristic maxim: paths leading to evil should be blocked (*sadd dhara'i'*). Thus all games are prohibited unless some benefit outweighs their detriment. For example, foot racing and wrestling are not forbidden because they are profitable for strengthening the body.

Going further, Ibn Taymiyya argues that God forbade *maysir* for more reasons than just gambling. Referring back to the Qur'anic text, he identifies the legal cause (*'illa*) of forbidding both *maysir* and wine as their corrupting and detrimental effects of enmity, hatred, and distraction from prayer and remembrance of God. Ibn Taymiyya identifies these same detriments in backgammon and chess, even when not played for stakes, and all the more so for chess. He first focuses on enmity and hatred. Chess players get so engrossed in their games that they do not even feel hunger and thirst. They do not take care of themselves and their families and they fail to pray and remember God. Their craving and addiction are often worse than that of wine drinkers, and their competitiveness leads to enmity, hatred, lying, and deceit. Ibn Taymiyya again invokes the maxim that paths leading to evil should be blocked, as well as the utilitarian principle of weighing up benefits and detriments. God has forbidden any act that leads to enmity, hatred, and detriment unless it involves some greater benefit. For example, a man should not be alone with a woman lest it lead to sin. However, one may eat carrion to avoid death because the detriment of death is worse than the detriment of eating something foul. When it comes to chess and backgammon, Ibn Taymiyya explains, there is no discernable benefit in these games, whereas the detriments are innumerable.

Ibn Taymiyya then adds his signature stamp to the argument by zeroing in on the worship-related causes of prohibition. Squandered wealth is completely secondary in the forbidding of *maysir*. The most fundamental cause of *maysir*, as well as wine and chess, being forbidden is its detriment to the intellect and the heart. The prayer and remembrance of God mentioned in the Qur'anic text forbidding wine and *maysir* belong to the heart. There is nothing more detrimental to the heart than blocking out prayer and remembrance of God and then tumbling into enmity and hatred. Ibn Taymiyya quotes the Qur'anic verse, "I did not create the jinn and humanity except that they might worship Me" (Q. 51:56), to underline the primacy of worship. Worship includes knowing, loving, and submitting to God. The foundation of that worship is the belief, knowledge, love, and fear of God found in the heart.

Ibn Taymiyya's fatwa on chess well illustrates his appeal to analogy and his independence from any one law school. The four Sunni law schools are relevant interlocutors, but they do not hold definitive authority. While Ibn Taymiyya concurs with the Hanbali prohibition of chess and sides with Malik Ibn Anas when needed, the argument itself stands solely on analogical reasoning from the Qur'an and the Sunna. In typically Taymiyyan fashion, it is also rooted in his moral concern to protect the human heart from obstacles to worship.

INVALIDATING TRIPLE DIVORCE

Ibn Taymiyya's trials over oaths on pain of triple divorce were narrated in Chapter Two. Here I will examine how he argues that three pronouncements of divorce count as only one. In his fatwa on forbidding chess, Ibn Taymiyya downplays differences among the Companions. His argument on divorce, however, highlights disagreement among the Companions in order to undermine the consensus alleged by his opponents. This clears the way for him to reconsider opposing hadith reports concerning the Prophet's Sunna.

There are several types of divorce in Islamic law. The type under consideration here is *talaq*, in which a man unilaterally divorces his wife. There are two ways to enact *talaq*: the proper way (*sunna*) and the innovated way (*bid'i*). Ibn Taymiyya and his contemporaries agree on how to enact a proper divorce. The husband is to issue one pronouncement of divorce when his wife is not menstruating. The second method of *talaq*, the innovated, is when the husband issues a pronouncement of divorce while the wife is menstruating, or between menstrual periods if sexual relations have already taken place in that interval. Mainstream Sunni jurists deemed an innovated divorce valid

– it effects a divorce – even though, confusing as it may seem, most of those same jurists forbade it. Ibn Taymiyya says that innovated divorce is both forbidden and invalid.

A single pronouncement of divorce is revocable. The man may return to his former wife and resume sexual relations. Once the husband divorces his wife three times on three different occasions, the divorce is irrevocable. The woman must marry and be divorced from another man before she can return to her first husband. The juristic consensus of Ibn Taymiyya's day also maintained that three pronouncements of *talaq* on one occasion effected a valid and irrevocable divorce. Ibn Taymiyya disagrees with this view. He argues that three pronouncements on one occasion count as only one pronouncement.

Ibn Taymiyya states that the Qur'an provides no grounds for the validity of triple divorce. He presents two hadith reports transmitted by the Companion of the Prophet Ibn 'Abbas to support his position. The first comes from the authoritative Sunni hadith collection of Muslim Ibn Hajjaj (d. 875):

> Ibn 'Abbas said, "Three pronouncements of divorce in the time of the Messenger of God, Abu Bakr, and the first two years of 'Umar's caliphate counted as one. 'Umar Ibn al-Khattab said, 'The people have started to act quickly in a matter in which they should show patience. If we impose [three pronouncements counting as three] upon them [it will dissuade them]... So, he imposed it upon them'."

The second hadith is found in the collection of Ahmad Ibn Hanbal:

> Ibn 'Abbas said, "Rukana...divorced his wife three times at once, and he was deeply saddened over her. The Messenger of God asked him, 'How did you divorce her?' He said, 'I divorced her three times'. [The Messenger of God] said, 'At once?' He said, 'Yes'. He said, 'That is only one. Return to her if you wish'. So, he returned to her'."

According to Ibn Taymiyya, these hadith reports show that the Prophet treated three pronouncements issued at one time as only one. His opponents grounded their view in 'Umar's precedent found in the first hadith, and they furthermore claimed that all the Companions had agreed with 'Umar. Ibn Taymiyya responds that 'Umar changed the law merely to deter men from making three pronouncements at once.

'Umar wanted to force men to suffer the consequences of their careless actions by losing their wives for good. Ibn Taymiyya allows that 'Umar had the right to enact this kind of discretionary punishment, but he also notes that some of the Companions disagreed with 'Umar, saying that this type of punishment was not permissible. 'Umar was not always right, he explains, and the Companions did not come to consensus around 'Umar's ruling. Ibn Taymiyya suggests that those who claim consensus for the validity of triple divorce are not aware of the opposing views among the Companions. That aside, he maintains that a consensus of the Companions around 'Umar's ruling would have been in error, as a consensus may not abrogate the Sunna of the Prophet.

The second hadith involving Rukana is clear that the Prophet counted three divorce pronouncements at once as only one. However, Ibn Taymiyya's opponents resorted to a different wording of this same hadith found in the collection of Abu Dawud (d. 889) which more easily suggested the validity of triple divorce. Ibn Taymiyya rejects the hadith in Abu Dawud as weak in its authenticity.

Ibn Taymiyya likewise dismisses the probative value of other incidents in the life of the Prophet that opponents invoked as evidence for their view. It was said that the Prophet did not object when three men – Rifa'a, 'Uwaymir, and the husband of Fatima bin Qays – issued triple divorce pronouncements. Ibn Taymiyya responds that Rifa'a and the husband of Fatima issued their three pronouncements on separate occasions in accord with proper practice. So their cases are not relevant. He also explains that 'Uwaymir first separated from his wife through a process of mutual cursing, which is a different kind of divorce process in Islamic law. 'Uwaymir triple divorced his wife only after that in order to emphasize the separation. Thus the case of 'Uwaymir is also irrelevant.

Ibn Taymiyya looks beyond the Sunna of the Prophet to make a number of other arguments. For example, he tries to show that a consensus of jurists on the validity of triple divorce never actually existed within Sunni Islam. He claims that his grandfather Majd al-Din (d. 1255), a prominent Hanbali jurist, was sometimes of the view that three divorce pronouncements at once counted as one. (There seems to be no evidence that Majd al-Din ever held this view.) Ibn Taymiyya additionally locates some Maliki opinions that accord with his own, and he states that the majority of the Zahiri law school agreed with him. The Zahiri school had died out by Ibn Taymiyya's day.

In a different line of defense, Ibn Taymiyya suggests that Sunnis may have succumbed to sectarian provocation. Shi'is maintain that three pronouncements at once count as only one. So some Sunnis may have felt compelled to distinguish themselves from Shi'is by asserting a consensus for the opposite view. Ibn Taymiyya does not think this sufficient reason to reject the witness of authoritative texts.

Ibn Taymiyya also marshals rational considerations for his case. He argues that it is contradictory to forbid triple divorce while yet treating it as valid and binding. To forbid it and simultaneously consider it valid defeats God's purposes in distinguishing the permissible from the impermissible. God prohibits certain acts to ward off their detriment. So making those acts legally binding nullifies God's purpose in prohibition. Moreover, some of his opponents deemed a triple divorce valid and irrevocable but still forbade the triple divorced woman from marrying and getting divorced from another man for the purpose of returning to her first husband. Ibn Taymiyya condemns this for causing great hardship, detriment, and enmity; it even leads people to apostatize from Islam. Ibn Taymiyya recognizes that some jurists permitted a triple divorced woman to marry and get divorced from another man intentionally to circumvent such problems, but he views this as equally problematic. There would be no need for such legal stratagems if God's law were followed properly in the first place.

In the end Ibn Taymiyya consigns the view of his opponents to the realm of erroneous independent reasoning. It is worthy of one reward from God for the effort but not two because it is wrong. The crux of the dispute is consensus. Ibn Taymiyya's opponents claimed that a consensus of the Companions had formed around 'Umar's ruling that three divorce pronouncements on one occasion produced a valid and irrevocable divorce. Ibn Taymiyya denies that this alleged consensus ever existed, and he adds that it goes against the Sunna of the Prophet. As in his ruling on chess, Ibn Taymiyya speaks on behalf of the Qur'an and the Sunna over against all other authorities. The Sunni law schools are worthy of respect, but Ibn Taymiyya claims to represent all of Islam on the strength of the revealed texts.

A number of Hanbali jurists adopted Ibn Taymiyya's ruling on triple divorce in the centuries after him. His introduction of this ruling into the Sunni legal tradition also greatly facilitated reform of divorce law in several modern Muslim states including Egypt, Jordan, and Morocco. More broadly, Ibn Taymiyya's appeal to the Qur'an and the Sunna against the authority of the Sunni legal school system has inspired a wide range of reform-minded Muslims over the last few centuries, and it distinguishes the contemporary Global Salafism movement from the many Sunnis who continue to adhere to a traditional legal school.

6

UTILITARIAN SOCIAL AND POLITICAL ETHICS

In November 1311 some rabble rousers assaulted Ibn Taymiyya in a Cairene mosque. Ibn 'Abd al-Hadi, Ibn Taymiyya's biographer who relates the incident, does not give any reason for the attack. Some of Ibn Taymiyya's followers offered to kill the perpetrators and destroy their homes. He held off his hot-headed enthusiasts, but they still thought the attackers had acted unlawfully and should be fought. Ibn Taymiyya countered that the altercation concerned no more than a matter of scholarly difference. He clearly was not interested in fighting over it. Ibn Taymiyya then insisted on returning to the mosque for the mid-afternoon prayer. His devotees protested that he could be killed, and demanded that he pray somewhere else. Nevertheless Ibn Taymiyya stubbornly proceeded to the mosque. Along the way, he passed by some people playing chess in front of a blacksmith's shop. He shook the chessboard and turned it over, leaving the players and bystanders dumbfounded. When Ibn Taymiyya arrived at the mosque people were murmuring that he would be killed. Ibn Taymiyya performed his prayers, and then he spoke about the disputed issue until the sundown prayer. Eventually, his opponents admitted that they had been wrong about him, and he departed unharmed.

In narrating these events, Ibn 'Abd al-Hadi no doubt accentuates the severity of the conflict to amplify Ibn Taymiyya's prudence and fortitude in calming the situation. Even so, Mamluk Cairo was fraught with social tension, and the threat of Mamluk military brutality lurked in the background. Had Ibn Taymiyya unleashed his enthusiasts against his attackers, a public disturbance would have ensued. Ibn Taymiyya would have lost favor with Sultan al-Nasir Muhammad for inciting a riot, and the other instigators would have suffered cruel punishment at the hands of the Mamluk authorities. Ibn Taymiyya would also have contravened his own conviction that public unrest was fundamentally detrimental to the common good.

Yet in the same account, Ibn Taymiyya put a violent end to a game of chess, a game he took to be prohibited, as we saw in the last chapter. He made his moral point forcefully, and he interfered in a matter normally reserved for government-appointed inspectors who regulated the markets and policed public morals. It was a vigilante act, but not one that would destabilize public order. Ibn Taymiyya believed it to be the responsibility of the Muslim community as a whole to judiciously ameliorate the religious condition of society. He took it to be his duty as a religious scholar to take the lead alongside the ruling authorities in achieving that end.

SOCIAL ETHICS

The religious basis of Ibn Taymiyya's social ethics is the Qur'anic injunction "to command the right and prohibit the wrong" (see e.g. Q. 3:104, 7:157, 9:71). Ibn Taymiyya finds the fullest expression of this interventionist injunction in jihad, which he says is better than prayer, fasting, and pilgrimage. Both jihad and commanding the right and prohibiting the wrong are collective obligations (*fard kifaya*). A collective obligation is incumbent upon the Muslim community as a whole, which means that some members of the community may fulfill the obligation on behalf of all the others. If no one performs these obligations, they become individual obligations for those capable of performing them.

However, along with the mainstream Sunni thinking of the time, it does not follow for Ibn Taymiyya that wrongdoing must be opposed in every instance. The world is far from perfect. An obsession with stamping out moral failure readily leads to even worse problems. One must instead consider the overall benefit and detriment of any intervention. As noted in Chapter Four, Ibn Taymiyya maintains that pure benefit coincides with following the prescriptions of the revealed law. Following the law is the path to maximum benefit. Yet the present condition of humanity is clearly corrupt, and attaining maximum benefit through perfect adherence to the law is not entirely possible. Thus one should commit deeds in which there is more benefit than detriment but avoid deeds in which there is more detriment than benefit. Ibn Taymiyya elaborates this as he addresses how to face moral ambiguity:

> One has to investigate. If the right is greater, it is commanded, even if it necessarily entails something wrong of lesser import. Wrong is not prohibited if [prohibiting it] necessarily entails losing something right greater than it. Indeed, prohibiting in that case would be tantamount to blocking the way of God... If the wrong is predominant, then it is prohibited, even if this involves losing something right less than it. Commanding that [lesser] right that involves a greater wrong is commanding wrong and furthering disobedience to God and His Messenger. If right and wrong are intertwined and equally in balance, then they are neither commanded nor prohibited. Sometimes it is beneficial to command, and sometimes it is beneficial to prohibit. Sometimes it is not beneficial to command or prohibit when the right and the wrong are intertwined. It all depends on the specific and actual circumstances. (MF 28:129–130, translation adapted from *Public Duties* 80–81)

As an example of benefits outweighing detriments, Ibn Taymiyya cites the Prophet indulging hypocrisy and immorality among some of his Companions who were otherwise fervent for his cause. If the Prophet had punished or even killed these Companions for their wrongdoing, he would have lost the greater good of their passion for Islam.

Conversely, according to Ibn Taymiyya, on balance civil war and insurrection against established authority are detrimental. This was also the view of medieval Sunni jurists more generally. It is better to have a sultan who is unjust than no sultan at all. To stress the point, Ibn Taymiyya cites the dictum, "Sixty years of an unjust sultan is better than one night without a sultan" (MF 20:54). He also criticizes the puritanical Khariji movement of early Islam for overzealousness in commanding the right and prohibiting the wrong. The Kharijis imagined that they were doing the will of God, but in fact they caused more detriment than benefit. This, Ibn Taymiyya explains, is why the Prophet commanded patience under injustice and prohibited fighting the governing authorities so long as they maintained ritual prayer.

A matter in which the balance of benefits and detriments can go either way for Ibn Taymiyya is emigration. The formative Islamic narrative of emigration is the Prophet Muhammad's flight in the year 622 from opposition in his hometown of Mecca to the town of Medina where he established his political and military authority. Ibn Taymiyya broadens the notion of emigration to include the moral senses of fleeing from sin and bad company and shunning sinners as a means of punishing them. Whether to flee sin or to shun sinners, Ibn Taymiyya counsels weighing up the benefits and detriments of emigration. Emigration of any kind should never lead to greater harm than the harm from which one is fleeing.

This utilitarian approach to emigration also helps make sense of the nuance in Ibn Taymiyya's short fatwa concerning the Muslims of Mardin, a religiously diverse town located today in southeastern Turkey (MF 28:240–241). Mardin had come under the rule of Mongol vassals in the late thirteenth century. The Mongols were not yet Muslims. Ibn Taymiyya was asked about the Islamic legal status of Mardin as a land of peace or a land of war. Mainstream medieval jurisprudence, broadly speaking, defined a land of peace, that is, a territory of Islam (*dar al-Islam*) as wherever Muslim rule and Islamic law prevailed. A land or territory of war (*dar al-harb*) fell under the control of unbelievers. Ibn Taymiyya was also asked whether Muslims should emigrate from Mardin to Islamic lands.

In response Ibn Taymiyya only requires emigration if the Muslims in Mardin can no longer practice their religion. Otherwise, emigration is recommended but not obligatory. Ibn Taymiyya furthermore explains that Mardin is neither a territory of peace nor a territory of war. It is a composite of the two. In the Mardin fatwa he appears to follow the mainstream definition of a territory of Islam. The territory of peace is where the army is Muslim and the rulings of Islam prevail. In other texts, however, Ibn Taymiyya defines territories as functions of the moral qualities of their inhabitants: "Whether a land is a territory of unbelief, a territory of belief, or a territory of bad sinners is not an attribute intrinsic to the [land itself] but an accidental attribute that depends upon its inhabitants" (MF 18:282). Back in the Mardin fatwa, Ibn Taymiyya likewise defines the territory of war as a function of its inhabitants. The territory of war is where unbelievers live. Mardin then is a composite (*murakkab*) territory because both believing Muslims and unbelievers live within it. While this situation is not ideal in Ibn Taymiyya's view, it is clearly bearable. It is not without preponderant benefit. Some revivalist Muslims today use Ibn Taymiyya's Mardin fatwa as inspiration for living peacefully in countries ruled by non-Muslims.

THE CALIPHATE

Ibn Taymiyya's thinking on the caliphate provides a further example of how he uses utilitarian reasoning to make the best of a morally imperfect situation. The caliphate was the foundation of Sunni Muslim political and legal authority throughout the pre-modern period, no matter how ineffectual individual caliphs may have been politically and militarily. It has been said that Ibn Taymiyya disregarded the caliphal institution completely, because he allegedly did not think it obligatory for the Muslim community to have a caliph. The caliphate had no basis in the Qur'an and the Sunna of the Prophet. This view of Ibn Taymiyya's thinking is not entirely correct. In a short undated treatise on the topic (MF 35:18–32), he maintains that the caliphate is indeed an obligation while at the same time exploring how to function without a true caliph.

Ibn Taymiyya's treatise on the caliphate deploys the usual categories of medieval Sunni political thought. He distinguishes between the caliphate (*khilafa*) on the one hand and kingship (*mulk*) on the other. The caliphate is the righteous rule of prophecy, while kingship is debased temporal power. For Ibn Taymiyya, the ideal "prophetic caliphate" (*khilafat al-nubuwwa*) corresponds to the first four "rightly guided" caliphs of Sunni orthodoxy: Abu Bakr, 'Umar, 'Uthman, and 'Ali in that order. (Shi'is place 'Ali first and regard the others as usurpers.) After these four, rule of the Islamic community degenerated into kingship. Ibn Taymiyya allows that kings may have been called caliphs thereafter, even when they did not attain to the perfection of the prophetic caliphate. He also maintains that the prophetic caliphate is always an obligation for the Muslim community. It is only permitted to forgo it in case of necessity. Kingship is a sin. It is blameworthy and subject to punishment.

Despite the caliphal obligation, Ibn Taymiyya shows no interest in the figurehead ʿAbbasid caliph in Cairo. The ʿAbbasid caliphs had ruled most of the Islamic world from 750 to the mid-900s from their capital Baghdad. Thereafter, invading powers deprived them of their political and military potency, and the caliphs confined themselves largely to religious and ceremonial roles. When the Mongol conquest of Baghdad in 1258 nearly wiped out the caliphate entirely, the Mamluks salvaged it by moving it to Cairo in 1261. The Mamluk sultan ruled primarily by force of political agility and military prowess, but he nonetheless used the caliph to bolster his Islamic legitimacy. This was achieved by having the figurehead caliph ceremonially delegate his Islamic political and legal authority to the sultan. Leading Shafiʿi jurists from al-Mawardi (d. 1058) down to Ibn Taymiyya's contemporary Ibn Jamaʿa developed legal stratagems to facilitate this delegation of authority from powerless caliphs to the de facto rulers of the day. Unlike al-Mawardi and Ibn Jamaʿa, Ibn Taymiyya does not speak of the need for a caliph to give legitimacy to the law and the sultan. He probably regards the Shafiʿi stratagems as empty legal fictions. For Ibn Taymiyya a real caliph will hold effective coercive power.

Back in his treatise on the caliphate, Ibn Taymiyya bridges the gap between the caliphal obligation and the absence of an ideal caliph by weighing up circumstances and treating kingship as no more than a minor sin (*saghira*). A king who commits many good deeds with just a few bad deeds mixed in is better than someone who does not take political responsibility at all. Ibn Taymiyya understands political responsibility to be part of religion. The pure and detached saint is of no benefit when there is governing to be done. It is the utilitarian calculus of benefits and detriments that should guide action in the social and political spheres.

This leads Ibn Taymiyya to discuss the general question of how to evaluate good deeds that include bad deeds as well. He says that this occurs in two ways. In the first, the evil deed is a necessary part of the good deed. The good deed cannot occur without the evil deed. In this case, Ibn Taymiyya explains, the evil deed is not actually evil. If the benefit of a good deed is greater than the detriment of the so-called evil deed, then the so-called evil deed is no longer forbidden. He gives the example of carrion. While eating carrion is normally prohibited, it is permitted if necessary to stay alive.

Ibn Taymiyya's second way that good and evil deeds combine involves a measure of indulgence. It might be humanly possible to perform a certain good deed, but it would be exceedingly arduous unless accompanied by something prohibited to ease the way. The prohibited deed is thus indulged to facilitate the good deed, as long as the benefit of the good deed outweighs the sinfulness of the evil deed. Ibn Taymiyya illustrates this phenomenon with examples pertaining to public leaders and religious scholars:

> An example is [the public leader] who cannot bring himself to achieve the benefits of administrative authority in commanding the right and prohibiting the wrong, carrying out prescribed punishments, securing the roads, undertaking jihad against the enemy, and distributing resources, without engaging in some prohibited things, like expropriating some of the resources, domineering the people, showing favoritism in distribution, and other such capricious behaviors. It is likewise in jihad. He is not able to bring himself to undertake jihad without a certain kind of rashness. [The scholar] is not able to bring himself to study the science of jurisprudence and the theological foundations of religion without certain kinds of prohibited things like [ungrounded] opinion and rationalist theology. And he cannot bring himself to study the science of the legislated rites of worship and the knowledge that is commanded without a certain kind of monkishness. (MF 35:30)

For Ibn Taymiyya a bit of rashness, favoritism, and expropriation of funds must be tolerated in public leaders to gain the benefits of their rule. The vices of religious scholars also deserve a measure of forbearance. In referring to monkishness, Ibn Taymiyya may well have had himself in mind. As noted in Chapter One, he never married. While he did regard marriage to be a Muslim duty, he may have chalked up his failure in this regard to the unfortunate costs of his scholarly vocation.

Ibn Taymiyya goes on in his treatise on the caliphate to give further examples of indulging rulers. One example involves a king who drinks wine even after converting to Islam. That king should not be prohibited from drinking, explains Ibn Taymiyya, if that prohibition incites him to apostatize. It is better that he should drink and stay Muslim so that he can support Muslim interests.

Despite this, Ibn Taymiyya maintains that there will be times when prohibitions must be made explicit to attain other objectives. Deciding when the time is right is again a matter of utilitarian calculation. This is in fact the way of the Prophet Muhammad, who expediently considered circumstances when making decisions. Ibn Taymiyya concludes, "Because of [the diversity of circumstances], the position of the Prophet varied regarding his command, his prohibition, his jihad, his pardon, his carrying out the prescribed punishments, his harshness, and his mercy" (MF 35:32).

To sum up Ibn Taymiyya's treatise, the Muslim community is obligated to fulfill the prophetic caliphate. However, no ideal caliph exists, and the Muslim community must make do with sinful kings whose rule brings far more benefit than harm. Ibn Taymiyya does not allow overturning prohibitions against things like eating carrion and drinking wine on a whim. However, he does think that it is not always possible to keep the law to perfection. It is thus necessary to do what most benefits the community in the overall circumstances. This is in fact the way of the Prophet, according to Ibn Taymiyya, and inasmuch as utilitarian reasoning is the very way of the Prophet, it is paradoxically the way to keep the law to perfection after all.

PUBLIC AUTHORITY AND THE LAW

Whether or not a true caliph exists, Ibn Taymiyya expects the public authorities to take the lead in commanding the right and prohibiting the wrong. He grounds public authority (*wilaya*) in both scripture and rational argument. As for scripture, he interprets "authorities" in the Qur'anic verse, "O you who believe! Obey God, and obey the Messenger and the authorities among you" (Q. 4:59), to include both religious scholars and military and political leaders. His rational argument begins with the premise that human beings are communal by nature. They need to cooperate to attain benefits in this world and in the hereafter. Humans need leaders who both command and prohibit with those ends in view and have sufficient power and authority to administer justice and establish religion.

In this more philosophical spirit, Ibn Taymiyya sometimes speaks of justice (*'adl*) as a kind of natural law. God supports justice wherever it is found, even among unbelievers. Ibn Taymiyya writes, "It is said, 'God gives victory to the just state, even if it is unbelieving, and He does not give victory to the unjust state, even if it is Muslim'... This is because justice is the order of everything. So, if the affairs of this world are maintained by justice, they will endure, even if he who is responsible has no share in the hereafter" (MF 28:146).

Of course, Ibn Taymiyya still believes that God sent the Prophet Muhammad with the best law and the best religion. The most perfect justice is found in following that law, and it is the purpose of public authorities to advance religion and promote worship of God alone. Furthermore, ruling is in itself a way of drawing near to God, even if most rulers selfishly aspire to gain wealth and control over others. Ibn Taymiyya disparages those who seek public authority for their own gain and abandon the priorities of religion. Yet he also censures those who withdraw from the public domain presuming to protect religion from the stain of corruption. Religion cannot do without temporal power.

Ibn Taymiyya thus writes of two degenerate paths with regard to religion and temporal authority: "the path of those aligned with religion who do not perfect it by means of what is needed in the way of temporal authority, war, and wealth, and the path of those who deploy temporal authority, war, and wealth and do not intend to establish religion thereby" (*Siyasa* 241). Following common medieval Muslim stereotypes, Ibn Taymiyya attributes the first path to Christians and the second to Jews, but he targets other Muslims as well. He derides the politically quietist leaders (*imams*) of Twelver Shi'ism for failing to produce historically tangible results, and he faces down the Shi'i charge that Sunni rulers were consumed with wine and immorality. He counters that Sunni leaders through the centuries achieved far more for religion than the Shi'i *imams*. Sunni rulers had admittedly committed many evil deeds, but they had also performed many good deeds that no one else could have done. They embarked on jihad, upheld public morals, brought justice, and imposed criminal penalties prescribed by the Qur'an and the Sunna of the Prophet.

These attacks on Christians, Jews, and Shi'is aside, Ibn Taymiyya is most fundamentally worried that effectual power and the revealed law had drifted too far apart in his own Mamluk society. The judges (*qadis*), who dealt largely with contracts and personal status cases, were usually understood to be the primary locus of the revealed law. While the sultan appointed these judges and enforced their judgements, he and his deputy governors also administered royal courts of their own, as we saw earlier in Ibn Taymiyya's trials in Damascus and Cairo. These royal courts dealt with complaints (*mazalim*) of diverse kinds, and they included among their officials one chief judge from each Sunni law school. However, the sultan was the final authority, and he meted out justice on the basis of his often brutal "public policy" (*siyasa*), a term that sometimes referred to little more than capital punishment as the tool of governance. On Ibn Taymiyya's reading, confining the revealed law to the domain of the judges was obscuring the law's wider relevance to public policy. The just public policy of the Prophet and early Muslim leaders had been forgotten. As a result, the revealed law had become ineffectual and the public policy of Muslim rulers capricious and despotic.

LAW-GUIDED PUBLIC POLICY

Ibn Taymiyya's solution to the problem of ineffectual law and tyrannical public policy is public policy guided by the revealed law. He sets this out in his well-known book of counsel for public authorities, *Law-*

Guided Public Policy (*Al-Siyasa al-shar'iyya*). As noted in Chapter Two, Ibn Taymiyya probably started writing this treatise in 1310 and completed it after returning to Damascus in 1313. The most influential precedent for this kind of treatise was *The Rules of Power* (*al-Ahkam al-sultaniyya*) by the eleventh-century Shafi'i jurist al-Mawardi. The aim of al-Mawardi's *Rules of Power* is to enfold government policy in the religious law and advise rulers on the religious law relevant to their affairs. In twenty chapters, al-Mawardi outlines the law pertaining to the caliph, his deputies, judges, complaints, administration of religious and bureaucratic affairs, punishment of crime, and the inspector of public spaces (*muhtasib*). Ibn Jama'a, Ibn Taymiyya's contemporary and the Shafi'i chief judge in Cairo, wrote a similar treatise called the *Digest of Rulings for the Administration of the People of Islam* (*Tahrir al-ahkam fi tadbir ahl al-Islam*). This book deals with the caliph, his deputies, administration of the revealed law, the military, jihad, and non-Muslims living under Muslim rule.

Ibn Taymiyya structures *Public Policy* differently from the works of al-Mawardi and Ibn Jama'a. Whereas the two Shafi'i jurists sketch out the formal requirements of specific public offices and administrative functions, Ibn Taymiyya divides his *Public Policy* more substantively into a part on public trusts and a part on justice. His basis for this division is the Qur'anic verse, "Truly, God commands that you render trusts to whom they are due, and that when you judge between people you judge with justice" (Q. 4:58). The first part of the book on public trusts further divides into a section on the trust of public office (*wilaya*) and a section on the trust of public wealth (*amwal*). The second part of the book treats justice toward God and justice between humans. For Ibn Taymiyya these matters of trust and justice together "comprise just public policy and effectual public authority" (*Siyasa* 6). Throughout *Public Policy*, he quotes copiously from the Qur'an and the hadith literature recording the Sunna of the Prophet in order to place public policy on the solid foundation of revealed law.

Trusts of public office and public wealth

In the section of *Public Policy* on the trust of public office, Ibn Taymiyya discusses the effective functioning of whatever public structures

Ibn Taymiyya also underlines here, as elsewhere, that exercising leadership is a religious obligation and that power is essential to establishing religion. He expresses deep confidence that the ruling authorities can reform the religious condition of their people. This is in fact a divinely ordained obligation incumbent upon both the military rulers and the religious scholars, not simply the religious scholars alone. Temporal authority and religion are inseparable for Ibn Taymiyya. All the affairs of this world find their proper ends in serving and supporting religion. The primary message of Ibn Taymiyya's *Law Guided Public Policy* is that religion is the public good toward which all exercise of authority in this world should be directed.

Jihad

As noted above, for Ibn Taymiyya jihad is the fullest expression of the duty to command the right and prohibit the wrong. The latter half of Chapter One traced his jihad activism and fatwa writing against the Mongols from 1299 to 1303. His fatwas against the Nusaryris and the Mongols-turned-Shi'is were discussed in the course of Chapter Two. At the end of Chapter Two, we also saw how Ibn Taymiyya interpreted all his diverse battles against grave visitation, the Mongols, the Ash'aris, the Sufis, and the people of Kisrawan as jihad. Ibn Taymiyya's notion of jihad thus extends well beyond the typical medieval juristic understanding of the duty as war against unbelievers. His notes on jihad in *Public Policy* provide a framework for this broader understanding.

Early in *Public Policy*, Ibn Taymiya gives jihad both inner and outer aspects. He observes that power in public offices is a matter of both self-control and control over others. He then links these two types of control to jihad against the self and jihad against external enemies, respectively. The jihad against the self echoes Sufi teachings about the greater jihad against the evil inclinations of the soul. Ibn Taymiyya writes,

> By means of the first power [i.e. self-control], a person is one of the emigrants who emigrate away from what God prohibits. He is one of the jihadis who fight jihad for God against themselves. This is the jihad against the inner enemy of Satan and caprice. By means of the second

> power [i.e. control over others], he is one of the emigrants fighting jihad in the path of God. They fight jihad against [God's] enemies. They support God and His Messenger. By means of them the religion is established. (*Siyasa* 36-37)

Further along in *Public Policy*, Ibn Taymiyya gives jihad against external enemies a distinctively penal coloring. He writes that the purpose of jihad is to "punish omission of duties and commission of forbidden acts" (*Siyasa* 97). Later in *Public Policy* Ibn Taymiyya elaborates on jihad against unbelievers (*kuffar*) under the rubric of the limits of God as punishments outlined above. Following standard medieval Muslim jurisprudence, he maintains that unbelievers outside the control of Islam should be invited to convert. If they do not respond, they must be fought in order to end discord and establish religion for God alone. Christians, Jews, and Zoroastrians are to be fought until they convert to Islam or submit to Islamic rule and agree to pay a poll tax (*jizya*). Going beyond the typical medieval doctrine, Ibn Taymiyya also calls for jihad against those who identify as Muslims but do not adhere to well-known laws of Islam. Although Ibn Taymiyya does not mention the Mongols in *Public Policy*, these are the grounds upon which he justifies fighting them in his anti-Mongol fatwas.

In further comments in *Public Policy*, Ibn Taymiyya explains that offensive jihad against unbelievers and those who refrain from some laws of Islam is obligatory at the collective level. That is, some Muslims must fulfill it on behalf of the whole community. Defensive jihad is obligatory for all Muslims who come under attack, as well as for other Muslims who can help them. During battle, women, children, monks, the elderly, and the disabled are not fought unless they engage in hostile activities. Ibn Taymiyya also cites the harsher juristic view that all unbelievers should be fought simply by virtue of their unbelief, with the women and children taken as war booty. He rejects this latter view, stating that "Fighting is only against those who fight us" (*Siyasa* 156). Unbelievers are to be left alone as long as they make no effort to spread innovation and unbelief. However, those who do attempt to spread their errant beliefs and practices must be fought.

Ibn Taymiyya's doctrine of jihad in *Public Policy* can appear uncompromising, but it is subject to pragmatic and utilitarian considerations.

He writes, "God permitted killing human beings as needed for the benefit (*salah*) of the people. God said, 'Discord is worse than killing' (Q. 2:217), which is to say, even if killing involves evil and detriment, the discord of the unbelievers involves even more evil and detriment" (*Siyasa* 159). For Ibn Taymiyya killing is justified to ward off the detriment of unbelief. However, as with commanding the right and prohibiting the wrong more generally, the overall purpose is benefit, and indiscriminate fighting and killing is of no benefit to Ibn Taymiyya's wider vision of law-guided public policy. Ultimately, for Ibn Taymiyya, the only thing worth going to war over is religion, and then only when it will bring preponderant benefit.

Modern Muslim literature taking inspiration from Ibn Taymiyya on "law-guided public policy" (*siyasa shar'iyya*) is plentiful. Some activists identify this term with an ideal Islamic political order. However, in his book *Law-Guided Public Policy* Ibn Taymiyya does not map out the perfect Islamic state. He instead calls on the public authorities to work within the existing political order to nurture religious reform prudently and gradually, and with force as necessary. More generally, in his social and political ethics Ibn Taymiyya seeks to uphold the revealed law and advance religious devotion to the extent possible. Following the law in its entirety is the path to maximum benefit, but when that full benefit is not attainable due to human weakness and moral failure, one must weigh up benefits and detriments and choose the most beneficial course of action in the circumstances.

This completes our survey of Ibn Taymiyya's spirituality and his views on religious, social, and political practices in Chapters Three through Six. The following two chapters examine Ibn Taymiyya's vision of what human beings should think about God and God's work with humanity. Among other things, this will show that God in Ibn Taymiyya's view likewise acts to promote benefit and religion to the fullest extent possible.

7

GOD AND CREATION

In Chapter Two we noted that Ibn Taymiyya's theological masterwork *Averting the Conflict* (*Dar' ta'arud*) came to eleven volumes in the published edition. Despite its size, *Averting the Conflict* makes up but a fraction of Ibn Taymiyya's theological corpus. Several other major works also deal extensively with God, God's relationship to the world, and prophethood. One of Ibn Taymiyya's disciples once asked him why he wrote more on theology than anything else. He responded that Islam had suffered much from innovation at the hands of philosophers, Sufis, and all sorts of wayward theologians and heretical groups. They had led people to doubt the foundations of their religion. It was his duty to counter specious arguments and clarify the true theological foundations of religion (*usul al-din*) from both reason and revelation. Ibn Taymiyya's theological work is a further expression of his wider campaign against innovation and his concern that God be worshipped rightly.

A key issue dividing Ibn Taymiyya and his opponents is how to interpret texts such as the Qur'anic verse, "The All-Merciful sat (*istawa*) over the Throne" (Q. 20:5). What does it really mean for God to sit over the Throne? Neither Ibn Taymiyya nor his adversaries affirm the plain sense (*zahir*) of the text without qualification, but they differ over what to affirm and what to negate. At the beginning of *Averting the Conflict*, Ibn Taymiyya arrays his opponents in three groups that I will call Kalam theologians, esotericists, and non-cognitivists. I will outline the interpretive strategy of each group in turn before exploring Ibn Taymiyya's own approach.

KALAM THEOLOGY

The term "Kalam theology" takes its name from the Arabic word *kalam*, meaning "speech." It came to denote the rationalist theology of the Mu'tazilis, Ash'aris, and others. Among Kalam theologians, Ibn Taymiyya's chief nemesis is the Ash'ari Fakhr al-Din al-Razi (d. 1210). Al-Razi's works contain diverse and sometimes contradictory views, but it was the kind of theology found in his *Compendium* (*al-Muhassal*) that enjoyed prominence in the early Mamluk Empire. Following the typical pattern of Kalam works, al-Razi's *Compendium* seeks to ground fundamental theological doctrines in reason, apart from revelation. Al-Razi first sets out his philosophical presuppositions, and then he proves the following with rational arguments: God exists; God does not have a body; God is not located, spatial, or subject to temporality; God has the attributes of power, knowledge, will, life, speech, hearing and sight; God is one; God wills all things and acts without purpose; and Muhammad was a prophet. With Muhammad's truthfulness as a prophet established by reason, the revelation in the Qur'an and the Prophet's Sunna may be trusted to supply further information about God, the afterlife, the nature of belief, and leadership of the Muslim community. However, revelation may not contradict reason, explains al-Razi, because it is only by reason that we know a messenger to be truthful. Reason must remain the arbiter of truth even when a trusted messenger informs us of something that opposes reason. The transmitted verbal reports of revelation cannot convey certain knowledge on their own.

Al-Razi thinks within a broad Hellenistic tradition of reason that rules out a corporeal God. "The All-Merciful sat over the Throne" cannot be taken in its literal sense because ascribing spatial extension, body, and motion to God is irrational. God is an existent that cannot be perceived by the human senses. God may not be said to be within the world, nor may He be said to be distinct from it. This leads al-Razi to prescribe a rule of interpretation that in his *Compendium* reads, "Either knowledge of [the literal sense of the text] is delegated to God, according to the doctrine of the Salaf... or [the literal sense] is reinterpreted perspicuously, according to the doctrine of most of the Kalam theologians" (*Muhassal* 158). The term "delegate" (*tafwid*) here means to entrust the meaning of the text to God and stop thinking about its implications in human language. To "reinterpret" (*ta'wil*) means to divert the text from its literal meaning to some other meaning deemed appropriate for God. In other words, al-Razi posits two steps for interpreting the literal senses of texts implying corporeality in God. The first is to deny that God has a body in accord with what reason requires. The second step is to choose between two further options. The way of the Salaf, the earliest Muslims, is to cease interpretation and delegate the meaning to God. The way of most Kalam theologians is to reinterpret the literal sense of the text non-literally. In *Establishing Sanctification* (*Ta'sis al-taqdis*), a thorough refutation of Hanbalis and others, al-Razi himself adopts the latter course. He reinterprets God's sitting (*istiwa'*) as God's vanquishing (*qahr*) and possessing (*istila'*).

Ibn Taymiyya criticizes al-Razi's rule of interpretation for stripping God of His attributes and making the Salaf out to be ignorant of the foundations of religion. Reinterpreting God's sitting as possessing strips God of His attribute of sitting. Attributing delegation to the Salaf deprives them of knowledge of the meaning of God's attributes. The Salaf did not simply transmit words only, that is, the verbal forms (*alfaz*) of God's attributes and then leave their meanings (*ma'ani*) to God. The Salaf knew and transmitted the meanings as well. Ibn Taymiyya's contemporary Ash'ari opponents took his criticism to heart and countered that delegation of meaning was not universal among the Salaf. Some of the Salaf had in fact engaged in reinterpretation.

More fundamentally, Ibn Taymiyya rejects the theological incorporealism that stands behind al-Razi's rule. He does not affirm explicitly that God is bodily and spatial because the terms body (*jism*) and spatial extension (*tahayyuz*) do not appear in the Qur'an or the sayings of the Prophet and the Salaf. He seeks to evade the charge of corporealism by reserving the label corporealist (*mujassim*) for those who affirm explicitly that God has a body. Nevertheless, he also does not deny that God is corporeal or spatial. Ibn Taymiyya is decidedly empiricist. He claims that nothing incorporeal and non-spatial exists outside the mind. Something existing outside the mind must be accessible to the human senses, and God is no exception. While God cannot be seen in this world, He can be seen in dreams, and He will be seen in the hereafter. Ibn Taymiyya's view of God raises questions about God's location and spatial extent, to which I will return below.

ESOTERICISM

Esotericists make up Ibn Taymiyya's second group of opponents. He ascribes esotericism in God's attributes to Isma'ili Shi'is, Sufis such as Ibn al-'Arabi, and philosophers like Avicenna (d. 1037) and Averroes (d. 1198), known in Arabic as Ibn Sina and Ibn Rushd respectively. We have already noted the esotericism of the Sufi Ibn al-'Arabi in Chapter Three. Avicenna's *Letter for the Feast of Sacrifice* (*al-Risala al-adhawiyya*) provides a philosophical example. The *Letter* explains that prophetic revelation depicts God and the rewards and punishments of the hereafter in terms of creaturely attributes for the benefit of the common people. The common people cannot bear the truth that God and the hereafter are incorporeal. The plain sense of Qur'anic revelation does not convey true knowledge of God and the afterlife, and the commoners should not be told that truth. Otherwise they may conclude that a God without a body does not exist at all. Only elite philosophers can grasp the true reality of God's incorporeality.

Ibn Taymiyya welcomes the fact that esotericists do not reinterpret verses like "The All-Merciful sat over the Throne" in the fashion of Kalam theology. He even adopts some of Avicenna and Averroes's key ideas, and he uses their arguments against non-literal reinterpretation to refute the Kalam theologians. However, Ibn Taymiyya rejects the esoteric claim that a higher truth lies behind the plain meaning of prophetic revelation. The God of esoteric speculation has no existence outside the mind. For Ibn Taymiyya prophetic revelation is not pious fiction. Its plain sense indicates the reality of God's existence and attributes.

NON-COGNITIVISM

The third group of Ibn Taymiyya's opponents comprises non-cognitivists who forbid thinking about the meaning of God's attributes. An example of non-cognitivism is Hanbali theologian Ibn Qudama's (d. 1223) treatise *Forbidding Study of the Books of the Kalam Theologians* (*Tahrim al-nazar fi kutub ahl al-kalam*). Ibn Qudama condemns Kalam theologians for inquiring into the meaning of God's sitting and then reinterpreting it as God's possessing. Such reinterpretation affirms one attribute that God did not affirm of Himself (possessing) while negating another attribute that He did affirm (sitting). Instead, Ibn Qudama contends, God must be described as He described Himself in the Qur'an and the Sunna of the Prophet recorded in hadith reports. The texts must be passed over (*imrar*) without comment and without inquiring into meaning (*ma'na*) or modality (*kayf*). The Qur'anic verse, "There is nothing like Him" (Q. 42:11) is sufficient to negate divine corporeality and similarity with creatures. The Salaf, Ibn Qudama continues, remained silent about the meanings of God's attributes and forbade reflecting on them. They transmitted the verbal forms of the attributes but not the meanings. There is in fact no need to know the meanings since no deeds depend on them. It is correct to believe in the attributes with ignorance.

APOLOGETIC INTERPRETATIVISM

Ibn Taymiyya's theology resembles Ibn Qudama's non-cognivitism in certain respects. God must be described as He describes Himself in the Qur'an and the Sunna. God is powerful, willing, loving, wrathful, laughing, and descending. God has a face and hands, and God is sitting over the Throne. The Kalam reinterpretation of God's sitting as possessing strips God of an attribute with which He has described himself. At the same time, God's attributes are unlike those of creatures except for their names, and the modalities of the attributes are unknown. The meanings, however, are known. Whereas Ibn Qudama says that both meaning and modality are unknown, Ibn Taymiyya distinguishes between the two.

Here is where Ibn Taymiyya diverges from the non-cognitivism of Ibn Qudama. He reproaches non-cognitivism for making the Salaf out to be ignorant of the foundations of the religion, the same charge that he levels against al-Razi's rule of interpretation. He insists that the Prophet and the Salaf transmitted not only the verbal forms of the revealed texts pertaining to God's attributes but also the meanings. The meanings are known, while their modalities are unknown. Passing over (*imrar*) the verbal forms of God's attributes for Ibn Taymiyya means leaving the meanings of their plain senses intact. It does not mean repeating the mere words without thinking about their meanings.

Ibn Taymiyya claims that the meanings of God's attributes are knowable so that he can compete with rivals in the theological fray. His approach is interpretative. The theological texts of the Qur'an and Sunna do in fact bring to mind thoughts about God. These thoughts must be guided in order to envision a God who is praiseworthy and to whom worship is due. Non-cognitivists too easily abandon the theological meaning of revelation to innovators with corrupt ideas. Ibn Taymiyya believes that the necessary response to the theological error of his day is not to shun it but to engage with it intellectually. The theologian's task is to clarify and defend the meaning of the revealed message transmitted by the Salaf in dialogue with the terminology and conceptual worlds of interlocutors. Ibn Taymiyya explains, "This requires knowledge of the meanings of the Book [i.e. the Qur'an] and the Sunna and knowledge of the meanings [intended by opponents] with the verbal forms, and then consideration of the two sets of meanings to make what agrees and what differs apparent" (*Dar'* 1:46). The technical terms of philosophy, Kalam theology, and Sufism may be used so long as they are given correct meanings congruent with the revelation. Even the Qur'an and the Sunna may be translated into other languages.

The boundary line in Ibn Taymiyya's mind between the meaning that is known and interpreted and the modality that is unknown is not entirely clear. Sometimes, the term "modality" marks off those questions and paradoxes that he does not wish to explore. At other times, the unknowability of modality serves as a reminder that all of God's attributes are in some sense unlike the attributes of creatures. They are all equally inscrutable. Either way, Ibn Taymiyya's aim is not to expose and explore theological issues for their own sake. Instead, his concern is practical. He seeks to refute competitors and articulate a theological discourse worthy of its subject, an understanding of God that gives God the highest worship and praise. Ibn Taymiyya's theology is part of his wider effort to spell out the law as the means by which God is to be loved and worshipped.

In line with this aim Ibn Taymiyya's interpretativism is also apologetic. Peppering his theological writings is the frequent refrain that reason does not contradict revealed tradition. This is the central claim of his *Averting the Conflict*. As noted in Chapter Four, this claim parallels Ibn Taymiyya's assertion that benefit and justice are coextensive with the revealed law. The basis of his confidence in the congruity of revelation and reason is his conviction that the Qur'an not only conveys information but also makes rational arguments. Revelation restates the essential rational proofs for God's existence, God's attributes, and God's messengers. Independent reason in turn recognizes those arguments as true. As I have written elsewhere (*Theodicy* 31), for Ibn Taymiyya "revelation embodies true rationality."

Ibn Taymiyya clarifies that the Qur'an does not use juristic analogies or categorical syllogisms in theological matters. A categorical syllogism is an argument of the form, "All humans are mortal; Socrates is a human; therefore, Socrates is mortal." Ibn Taymiyya accepts that a categorical syllogism yields certain knowledge when its premises are certain. We also saw in Chapter Five that he uses analogies in matters of religious practice. However, he asserts, analogies and syllogisms are not used in theological discourse because they compare God and creatures directly.

Ibn Taymiyya explains that the Qur'an respects the radical difference between God and the world by using a fortiori argumentation. An a fortiori argument concludes from a weaker case (e.g. human beings) that something applies with all the more reason to a stronger case (e.g. God). Ibn Taymiyya cites several Qur'anic examples, of which one will suffice here. The Qur'an states,

> [The pre-Islamic idolaters] assign daughters to God – Glory be to Him – and to themselves what they desire. When one of them is given news of a girl, his face becomes dark, and he chokes inwardly… Shall he

> keep her with dishonor or bury her in the earth? Certainly, evil is their decision. For those who do not believe in the hereafter is a similitude of evil, and to God is the highest similitude… They assign to God what they hate." (Q. 16:57–62)

While this text condemns the idolaters for female infanticide, it still implies a negative view of daughters, although the Qur'an denies as well that God had a son. The theological a fortiori argument in this Qur'anic passage proceeds as follows. If having daughters is judged to be an imperfection in humans, then with all the more reason daughters should not be attributed to God. Only the "highest similitude" or, in the terminology of the philosophized theology of Ibn Taymiyya's time, the "highest perfection" should be ascribed to God.

Ibn Taymiyya restates God's right to perfection (*kamal*) as a general principle. God is all the more worthy of being qualified with perfections found in creatures than are the creatures themselves, and God is all the more worthy of being exonerated of imperfections found in creatures than are the creatures themselves. This fundamental principle, Ibn Taymiyya claims, is known not only from the Qur'an and the Sunna but also by reason and the human natural constitution (*fitra*). The rational principle of causal priority dictates that a cause is more perfect than its effect. Thus the Creator as cause is necessarily more perfect than the creature as effect. Moreover, creatures derive all of their perfections from their Creator. So God is a fortiori worthy of the perfections found in them. On this basis Ibn Taymiyya derives a large number of divine attributes through rational argument rooted in his particular vision of perfection. He does this without direct reference to the Qur'an and Sunna. The following is an example:

> If [God] were not living, knowing, hearing, seeing and speaking, it would necessarily follow that He is dead, ignorant, deaf, blind and mute. He must be exonerated of these imperfections. Indeed, He – Glory be to Him – has created whoever is living, hearing, seeing, speaking, knowing, powerful and moving. So, He is all the more worthy to be like that. Indeed, every perfection in a caused, created thing is from the perfection of the Creator. (MF 8:21, translation adapted from *Theodicy* 64)

Ibn Taymiyya says that God is moving (*mutaharrik*) because, as he argues, a God who could not move on His own initiative would be inferior to creatures who can so move. Ibn Taymiyya also argues that laughter and joy are attributed to God in order to rule out the imperfections of crying and sadness. Furthermore, God has hands because one who has power to act with his hands is superior to one who does not have that option. Ibn Taymiyya exonerates God of the imperfections of eating and drinking on the grounds that God has no need to take anything into Himself. Ultimately, explains Ibn Taymiyya, God is ascribed with the highest imaginable perfections, and the pinnacle of those perfections is to be unlike creatures. A God not qualified with such perfections would not be worthy of praise and worship.

GOD IS SITTING OVER THE THRONE

Ibn Taymiyya's treatment of God's sitting over the Throne in his 1298 *Hamawiyya* and later texts amply illustrates the interpretive and apologetic aspects of his theology. He maintains that the Throne was created before the heavens and earth as we know them. God's sitting over the Throne must be affirmed in its plain sense, but in a way uniquely befitting God and without inquiring into modality. Sitting may not be reinterpreted as possessing. Beyond that, Ibn Taymiyya is not very interested in exploring whether God touches the Throne and such like, but he does have to confront an apparently contradictory Qur'anic claim. How does God's sitting over the Throne fit with the Qur'anic affirmation that God "is with you wherever you are" (Q. 57:4)? Kalam theologians like al-Razi said that God cannot be both literally over the Throne and literally with us in the world wherever we are. God's sitting over the Throne cannot be interpreted literally. Ibn Taymiyya disagrees. His interpretation involves three steps.

First, Ibn Taymiyya rejects literalism as a theory of meaning. It is technically incorrect to call Ibn Taymiyya a literalist, as is often done. In the literalist theory of meaning predominant in medieval Islam, each word possesses a literal sense that attaches to it when devoid of context. Then it takes on additional senses when contextual factors divert the literal meaning to non-literal meanings. The literal sense of "lion", for example, is a large and ferocious cat. Calling a fearless man in battle a "lion" is to divert the term to a non-literal sense. Ibn Taymiyya articulates instead a pragmatic or contextual theory of meaning. Words do not have literal meanings. Their meanings depend entirely on context. A word stripped of context has no meaning. Someone hearing the word "lion" always requires contextual indicators to tell whether a large cat or a fearless man is meant.

Second, Ibn Taymiyya establishes the context of God's sitting over the Throne. As noted earlier, he does not affirm explicitly that God is a body or spatially extended because such terms do not appear in the Qur'an, the Sunna, and the sayings of the Salaf. However, he does state that it is known with certainty by revelation, reason, and the human natural constitution that God is located above (*fawq*) and over (*'ala*) all things. He supports this with many Qur'anic texts such as, "They fear the Lord above (*fawq*) them" (Q. 16:50), "The All-Merciful sat over (*'ala*) the Throne" (Q. 20:5), and "The angels and the Spirit ascend to him" (Q. 70:4), as well as hadith reports like, "God is over His Throne, and He knows what you are doing." Ibn Taymiyya argues that such texts are so numerous that they provide certain knowledge that God is above and outside the created world. Moreover, Ibn Taymiyya argues rationally, if God were in the world, He would come into contact with all manner of dirt and filth found within it. That would be unworthy of God.

Third, having established this context, Ibn Taymiyya explains that the plain sense of God's "withness" in the verse "[God] is with you wherever you are" is clearly not spatial proximity. We already know that God is not in the world but over and above it. So the plain sense of "with" is then God's knowledge of our circumstances. Reading "withness" as God's knowledge is not a matter of reinterpreting "with" non-literally, as Kalam theologians would have it. It is instead the plain sense of "withness" dictated by the context in which it is expressed. Ibn Taymiyya suggests that this is perhaps as when a man speaks of the moon and the stars being with him while travelling by night, or when a father sitting on a roof tells his crying son on the ground below not to be afraid because he is with him. Ibn Taymiyya is careful to indicate that his exploration of meaning is not a matter of likening and assimilating God to creatures. The modality remains unknown. It is rather a matter of speaking about God in the most praiseworthy fashion in accord with the Qur'anic dictum, "To God is the highest similitude" (Q. 16:60).

Fakhr al-Din al-Razi in *Establishing Sanctification* mocks the idea that God is above and over the world. He argues that God is incorporeal, non-spatial, inaccessible to the human senses, and neither inside the world nor distinct from it. As noted in Chapter Two, Ibn Taymiyya wrote *Explication of the Deceit of the Jahmiyya* (*Bayan talbis al-Jahmiyya*) during his first imprisonment in Egypt to refute al-Razi's book.

Ibn Taymiyya's responses to two of al-Razi's many arguments will illustrate his rational defense. They also exemplify how Ibn Taymiyya engages the technical terminology of Kalam theology. In the first argument, al-Razi claims that God cannot be located above every part of the earth. The earth is spherical. If God happened to be located above those people living on the eastern part of the earth, God would be below those living on the western part. This being absurd, God cannot be located. Ibn Taymiyya counters that people say that God is above the sky no matter where they stand on the spherical earth. People living on the eastern part of the earth do not say that God is below those living on the western part. The direction below does not apply. In a different treatise Ibn Taymiyya indicates that God's Throne and the heavens below it are exceedingly small relative to God. To emphasize the point, he quotes the Qur'anic verse, "The whole earth will be in His grip on the Day of Resurrection, and the heavens will be rolled up in His right hand" (Q. 39:67). Ibn Taymiyya explains that the whole world in the hand of God is smaller than a chick pea in one of our hands. With such an image in mind, it is not difficult to imagine God located above a spherical earth from any point on its surface because God completely surrounds it.

In a second argument, al-Razi asserts that a corporeal God accessible to the human senses would have to be the size of the tiniest particle. Anything bigger would be divisible into its composite parts. A God made of parts would violate God's unity. Therefore, God is obviously neither corporeal nor spatial. Ibn Taymiyya denies that a large God would be divisible into separate parts. Something can be both indivisible and large. If God is a spatially extended existent located above His Throne, this does not mean that God can be divided up into parts located in distinct spaces. Moreover, Ibn Taymiyya explains, even the Ash'aris, including al-Razi, allow for a measure of distinction and differentiation within God by affirming multiple attributes. If a diversity of real attributes within the essence of God does not render God divisible, then spatial extension in God does not render God divisible either.

Ibn Taymiyya is profoundly reticent to speak of body and spatial extension in God. The terms are not Qur'anic. Ibn Taymiyya cites with approval Averroes's observation that the texts of revelation are silent as to whether God has a body. Yet when Ibn Taymiyya does use the technical terms of Kalam theology to engage al-Razi, he affirms that God is a very large being who completely surrounds the universe. This fits with the Qur'anic image of God holding the heavens and the earth in His hand.

Ash'ari and Shi'i polemicists through the centuries have condemned Ibn Taymiyya for corporealism. The charge of corporealism also landed him in prison in Cairo in 1306. While it is well-nigh impossible to find Ibn Taymiyya affirming that God has a body explicitly, there is substantive basis for the charge. Later figures like the Sufi Ibrahim al-Kurani (d. 1690) have tried to defend Ibn Taymiyya by assimilating his view to the delegation (*tafwid*) position attributed to the Salaf in al-Razi's rule. However, Ibn Taymiyya does not deny the corporeality of God outright, as al-Razi's rule requires. Instead, he posits a God of enormous size who encompasses the universe. As we shall see next, this God is also ever creative and ever active in a temporal sense.

THE TIMELESSLY ETERNAL GOD OF PHILOSOPHY AND KALAM

Ibn Taymiyya's view of God is dynamic. He maintains that God wills on account of causes or wise purposes that subsist in God's essence. Moreover, God creates perpetually by His will and power from eternity. These doctrines mark Ibn Taymiyya off from the mainstream of

Islamic philosophers and Kalam theologians. While those philosophers and Kalam theologians differ over the relation of purpose to God's will, they all agree that God is timelessly eternal. A survey of their arguments will set the stage for Ibn Taymiyya's own view.

The Ash'ari Kalam theologians deny purpose and causality in God's will for three reasons. First, purpose would introduce imperfection and need into God. Those performing acts for purposes are perfected by them. If God willed to act for a purpose, God would be imperfect prior to the act and then perfected by it. Second, it would introduce temporality into God's essence. If God willed and acted for a purpose, God would change through time as He fulfills His purposes. God would become a substrate for temporally originating events (*hawadith*). Third, purpose would introduce an infinite regress of causes into God's essence. Each purpose or cause would require a prior purpose or cause to bring it into existence, and this would lead to a chain of causes back into the infinite past. To avoid all of these problems, the Ash'aris affirm that seven eternal and essential attributes subsist in God's timeless essence. These are life, knowledge, will, power, speech, hearing, and sight. It is in the very nature of God's eternal will to assign the point at which God began to create without introducing any change or temporality in God. The impossibility of an infinite regress also precludes the eternity of the world. The world had a beginning.

Mu'tazili Kalam theologians and those Shi'is who follow them agree that the world had a beginning. They also concur that God is timeless in His essence. However, they accuse the Ash'aris of making God out to be vain and foolish by denying purpose in God's will. They affirm instead that God wills and acts for purposes, but purposes disjoined from God's essence. God acts for the purposes of benefiting humanity, but those purposes do not introduce change or need in God because they are located outside God. God gains nothing from them. The Ash'aris countered that even purposes disjoined from God necessarily impact God in some way. A God who acts for purposes outside His essence is still subject to temporality and is lacking in self-sufficiency.

Islamic philosophers fault the Kalam theologians for thinking that God could will to create the world without temporal origination arising in God's essence. Temporal events in the world cannot originate without a cause originating in God's will. Philosophers evade the Kalam problem by explaining the world as the eternal effect of an eternal cause. In the Neoplatonism of Avicenna, God is pure, simple, unchanging perfection. Any change in God would introduce imperfection into God. God in His eternal perfection is also productive and so eternally emanates the world. Being simple and perfect, Avicenna's God does not act for purposes, and this God does not create for the benefit of the world. The world flows not from God's love for the world but from God's love for Himself. God's will is not a matter of choosing between alternatives but choosing what God already knows and does. God is the sole origin of the world and, being the only world that the perfect God can emanate, it is necessarily the best possible.

GOD WILLS FOR WISE PURPOSES AND CREATES FROM ETERNITY

Ibn Taymiyya complains that philosophers like Avicenna reduce God's will to God's knowledge. He also rejects Avicennan emanationism. A timelessly eternal God could never give rise to the temporality of this world. For the same reason, Ibn Taymiyya agrees with the philosophers that the timelessly eternal will of the Kalam God can never begin to originate the world without a temporal cause originating. According to Ibn Taymiyya, God creates on account of causes and wise purposes that activate God's will and power. God acts, speaks, and creates by His will and power. A timelessly eternal will is as good as no will at all. Ibn Taymiyya roots this in God's perfection and Qur'anic argument: "Acting is an attribute of perfection...He – Exalted is He – has said, 'Is then He who creates as one who does not create? Will you not then remember?' (Q. 16:17). That being the case, it is reasonable that the agent who acts by his power and his will is more perfect than one having no power and no will" (*Minhaj* 1:371, trans. *Theodicy* 87).

Ibn Taymiyya's position entails temporally originating events subsisting in God's essence. He has no difficulty with this, and he asserts that it is the position of the Salaf. Yet, he prefers to speak of God's "voluntary attributes" (*al-sifat al-ikhtiyariyya*) and "voluntary acts" (*al-af'al al-iktiyariyya*) instead of "originating events" (*hawadith*) because the former terms are closer to the expression of the Qur'an and the Sunna. That aside, the idea that originating events subsist in God's essence was not new to the Islamic tradition. Ibn Taymiyya knew about it directly from Fakhr al-Din al-Razi. Al-Razi maintained the traditional Ash'ari doctrine of God's timelessness throughout most of his life. Then, as Ibn Taymiyya himself points out, al-Razi argues in his late work *Sublime Issues* (*al-Matalib al-'aliya*) that originating events in God's essence is the logically necessary position for all theological groups. It follows from God's knowledge of changing events occurring in the world that God's knowledge itself changes. God does not hear words until they are spoken or see a picture until it exists. God's will to originate also involves temporal origination in God Himself. Al-Razi does not integrate the import of these arguments into his wider theology, but Ibn Taymiyya does.

Ibn Taymiyya has no problem with an infinite regress either. He refutes the Kalam arguments against an infinite series, and he affirms an infinite regress of acts in God's essence: "[God] has been active from eternity when He willed with acts that subsist in His self by His power and His will one after another" (*Minhaj* 1:146, trans. *Theodicy* 81). Likewise, God in His perfection has been creating one thing or another from eternity (*min al-azal*). God's creative acts have no beginning, but every created thing has had a beginning. Following the Kalam theologians, Ibn Taymiyya maintains that every created thing came into existence after not having existed. While there have always been created things of one sort or another, no one created thing is eternal. The genus or species of created things is eternal, as Ibn Taymiyya puts it, but each individual thing has had a beginning.

Ibn Taymiyya's view of God's continuous creation of the world is similar to that of Averroes, and he was aware of Averroes's writings on the matter. Both Averroes and Ibn Taymiyya reject Avicenna's emanation scheme. Both also observe that the Kalam account of creation of the world out of nothing with a beginning violates the plain sense of the revealed texts. The Qur'an does not say that the world had a beginning. It only says that this present world was created in the context of a prior created existence, a world that included water and God's Throne:

"[God] created the heavens and the earth in six days, and His Throne was on the water" (Q. 11:7). The Qur'an also indicates that this world was created out of prior matter: "[God] rose toward the heaven when it was smoke, and He said to it and to the earth, 'Come willingly or unwillingly'. They both said, 'We come, willingly'" (Q. 41:11). From this, and on the basis of God's perfection, Ibn Taymiyya affirms that God's world of created things extends infinitely into the past.

Like the Mu'tazilis, Ibn Taymiyya affirms that God acts for wise purposes. However, he does not affirm this in Mu'tazili fashion. The Mu'tazilis attempt to absolve God of need and temporal change by disjoining God's purposes from God's essence and insisting that God only acts for the benefit of creatures. God does not act for His own benefit. According to Ibn Taymiyya, this not only strips God of His wise purposes but also makes God indifferent to His creatures. Rational agents necessarily take interest in the benefit and praise that redound to them for their actions. Ibn Taymiyya explains, "Anyone who commits an act in which there is neither pleasure, nor benefit, nor profit for himself in any respect, neither sooner nor later, is aimless, and he is not praised for this" (MF 8:89–90). For Ibn Taymiyya, God acts on account of wise purposes subsisting in God's essence that redound to both creatures and God Himself. Ibn Taymiyya's God is self-interested and utilitarian in much the same fashion as human beings.

This brings Ibn Taymiyya squarely up against the Ash'ari criticism that purpose in God's will subjects God to imperfection and need. A God who acts for wise purposes is imperfect prior to His act and perfected by performing it. Ibn Taymiyya counters by reinterpreting God's self-sufficiency along Avicennan lines. For the Ash'aris the world is irrelevant to God's self-sufficiency. God is fully God whether God creates a world or not. For Ibn Taymiyya the world is intrinsic to God's perfection. God has always been creating one thing or another. So God's self-sufficiency does not mean indifference to the existence of the world. It means instead that God needs no help in the act of creating. God is the sole and self-sufficient originator of the world and all that occurs within it.

Ibn Taymiyya also deploys the Avicennan notion of God's self-love to explain God's self-sufficiency. God loves the worship and obedience of His servants in the world. However, God does not create the world out of love for that worship and obedience, at least not in the first instance. Instead, the world follows on secondarily from God's love for Himself, which is primary and fundamental. Ibn Taymiyya writes, "What God loves of worship of Him and obedience to Him follows from love for Himself, and love of that is the cause of [His] love for His believing servants. His love for believers follows from love for Himself" (MF 8:144, trans. *Theodicy* 99). Moreover, God's love and praise of Himself so greatly exceeds human love and praise of Him that He does not need the latter. Indeed, it is God Himself who creates the human love and praise.

As well, Ibn Taymiyya responds to the Ash'aris that those who do things for wise purposes are obviously more perfect that those who act without purpose. Perfection is to do things when wise purposes require and not arbitrarily and haphazardly. To act when wisdom does not require is an imperfection. Also, a God perfected by His acts is no different from a God perfected by His attributes. God's acts are just as much necessary concomitants of God's perfection as His attributes are. Ultimately, for Ibn Taymiyya, it is the God of philosophy and Kalam theology that is imperfect. The perfect God creates by His will and power from eternity for wise purposes. Any other God would not be worthy of praise and worship.

8

GOD AND HUMANITY

Chapters Three and Seven together introduced many essentials of Ibn Taymiyya's theological framework. He maintains that the following doctrines are known by revelation on the one hand and reason and the human natural constitution on the other. God exists. God possesses attributes of perfection. God is above the created world. God creates all things for wise purposes that both redound to Him and benefit His creatures. God creates humans as loving and worshipping beings, ever seeking benefit and repelling harm. God naturally constitutes human beings to find their fullest benefit in worshipping Him alone, and they will indeed worship God as long as no impediments interfere. God sent prophets to complete and perfect the human natural constitution. God likewise gave the law for the wise purpose of guiding humanity to maximum benefit through worship of Him alone.

This chapter explores how Ibn Taymiyya understands God's moral relation to humanity. Despite his immense optimism in the goodness of God and the human inclination to worship God, it is nonetheless evident to Ibn Taymiyya that humans fail to fulfill the purposes for which God naturally constituted them. If God wills and creates everything that exists for wise purposes, then what does Ibn Taymiyya make of injustices, evils, and sins? In a world of lies and deception, how does one distinguish the true prophet and the correct religion from the false? Will there ever come a time when God's intention for humanity is fulfilled in full?

JUSTICE, EVIL, AND THE HUMAN ACT

The problem of God's justice in Islamic theology is straightforward. If God creates an act of human disobedience, how could God be just to prohibit and punish it? The Mu'tazili Kalam theologians resolve this by making humans the creators of their own acts. Humans commit their acts free of external determinants. God does not interfere in the human choice to commit good or bad deeds. God is therefore just to reward good deeds and punish bad deeds. Both the Ash'aris and Ibn Taymiyya reject the Mu'tazili solution as denying the exclusive power of God. It is God who creates human acts. Both the Ash'aris and Ibn Taymiyya also accuse the Mu'tazilis of holding God hostage to human standards of justice. God does not need to adhere to human notions of fairness in the distribution of rewards and punishments. The Ash'aris argue that God has the right to do with His creation as He sees fit. God would be just to punish even those who obey Him. Humans know that God will not do that, according to the Ash'aris, only because God has said that He will not. Ibn Taymiyya retorts that the Ash'ari God cannot be trusted to keep His word. A God who does not act for wise purposes is capricious. Instead, Ibn Taymiyya asserts, it is known necessarily that God creates all things for wise purposes. God's justice consists in God putting everything in its proper place according to those wise purposes. The way things are is good and perfect. This, however, begs the question of why things are not better than they are. Ibn Taymiyya gives deeper reflection to the matter in discussions on evil.

Ibn Taymiyya addresses evil as both a challenge to God's goodness and a problem of human responsibility. With respect to God, he echoes the Neoplatonism of Avicenna in providing three types of explanation. First, everything that God creates is fundamentally good in itself. Evils are only evil relative to creatures. Ibn Taymiyya writes, "[God] does not create pure evil. Rather, in everything that He creates is a wise purpose by virtue of which it is good. However, there may be some evil in it for some people, and this is partial, relative evil" (MF 14:266, trans. *Theodicy* 183).

Second, a measure of evil is necessary in the expression of God's perfection and the creation of the best possible world. In a treatise that is probably from late in his life, Ibn Taymiyya affirms a dictum that goes back to al-Ghazali: "There is nothing in possibility more wonderful than what is" (JR 142). In earlier writings Ibn Taymiyya had criticized this dictum for limiting God's power to do other than what God does. The dictum appears to say that God could not have created anything else. However, Ibn Taymiyya eventually defends the dictum. God could have created something else, but God in His wise purpose created this world because it was the best possible.

Third, and again resembling the philosopher Avicenna, Ibn Taymiyya emphasizes that the amount of evil in the world is minuscule in comparison to the great amount of good. The benefit in rain, for example, far outweighs the inconvenience and damage that it causes for some people. Prophets bring benefit to humanity as a whole that far exceeds the humiliation and death that they might visit upon unbelievers.

At the level of human responsibility, Ibn Taymiyya deploys two different strategies. First, following the philosophically inflected Kalam theology of his time, he affirms that God creates by means of secondary causes. God creates burning by means of fire, plants by means of rain, price rises by means of injustice, children by means of sexual intercourse, illness by means of poison, and human acts by means of human will and power. The exercise of human will and power distinguishes voluntary acts from the involuntary. God is fully the creator of both kinds of acts, including the will and the power for voluntary acts. However, God is just to reward and punish voluntary acts by virtue of the fact that He creates them in human beings and not in Himself. Human acts belong to human beings and not to God, just as the hair that God creates on human heads belongs to humans and not to God. Ibn Taymiyya sometimes runs into difficulties with this defense of human responsibility. To find a way out he resorts to his theological principle of God's a fortiori right to perfection. Consider the case of a master's servant in whom God creates injustice. According to Ibn Taymiyya, if it is just for the human master to punish his servant for that injustice, then it is all the more just for God to punish that same servant.

Ibn Taymiyya deploys a second and apparently later strategy for attributing evil to human beings in his treatise *The Good Deed and the*

Evil Deed (MF 14:229–425). Here, he turns to the Avicennan and Neoplatonic notion that evil is the absence or privation of good. Ibn Taymiyya locates the source of evil in human ignorance and the failure of humans to do that for which they were created. Both this ignorance and this failure have no existence and are therefore not things created by God. God does create sins in people and then punish them for those sins, but God creates those sins justly as punishment for an original failure to do the good deeds that God created humankind to perform. God is not responsible for that original failure because He did not create it. It is a nonexistent for which human beings alone bear responsibility. Yet why does God create human beings weak so that they fail to do good deeds? Ibn Taymiyya again turns to God's wisdom. God in His wise purpose creates human beings susceptible to moral failure.

Ibn Taymiyya does not always reveal God's wise purposes in evil. Sometimes he says that they cannot be known and that God is not to be questioned. At other times, though, he provides religious reasons for God's creation of evil. Human sins and their destructive consequences serve to instruct and deter others. Adversity, sickness, and oppression expiate sins and engender repentance, patience, humility, softening of the heart, and calling out to God. In fact some of these spiritual qualities would not be possible without evil and sin. Ibn Taymiyya writes, "A sin necessitates a servant's humility, his subjection, invocation of God, his asking Him for forgiveness and his bearing witness to his poverty and to his need for Him and that no one can forgive sins except Him. Because of the sin, good things happen to the believer that would not have happened without this" (MF 14:318–319, trans. *Theodicy*, 193).

For Ibn Taymiyya evil is fundamentally a matter of divine training. God creates evil to purify and educate human beings into religious virtue and worship of God alone. Sufis see evil in similar fashion as God's instrument of discipline on the spiritual path. This therapeutic and educational interpretation of evil colors Ibn Taymiyya's view of Hell-Fire, as we will see in the last section of this chapter, as well as his understanding of God's protection of prophets from sin and error, which is discussed next.

GOD'S PROTECTION OF PROPHETS

It is a basic Islamic conviction that God protects prophets from sin and error in conveying the divine message. Shi'is uphold the complete sinlessness or impeccability of the Prophet Muhammad, as well as their inspired leaders, the *imams*, who came after him. Sunnis today may allow that Muhammad committed some minor mistakes or sins, but they insist that he was infallible (*ma'sum*) in his transmission of the Qur'an. This was likewise the majority Sunni position at the time of Ibn Taymiyya. Ibn Taymiyya himself, however, follows a minority view that was more common earlier on. Prophets may err and sin, even in matters concerning revelation, but God protects them by making sure that their errors and sins do not become permanent. The Prophet Muhammad committed mistakes and sins, but he always repented and did not persist in them.

Ibn Taymiyya puts a point on this doctrine by accepting the controversial story of the Satanic Verses as historical and using it to underscore the value of Muhammad's repentance. Early Qur'an commentaries and accounts of the Prophet's life relate the story. It takes place during Muhammad's early ministry in Mecca. Some Muslims had emigrated to Abyssinia (Ethiopia today) to escape persecution by the Meccans. One day, Muhammad was reciting the Qur'an in the presence of Meccan polytheists. After naming three Arabian goddesses (Q. 53:19–20), he added two more verses, "These are the high-flying cranes whose intercession is to be hoped for." The polytheists thought Muhammad had accepted their goddesses, and the two sides reconciled momentarily. The émigrés in Abyssinia heard about the reconciliation and started to return home. However, the angel Gabriel informed Muhammad in a revelation that Satan had added the additional two verses. Muhammad was disturbed, and Gabriel gave him the following verse to comfort him, "We never sent a messenger or prophet before you except that when he was yearning [for a revelation], Satan threw [something] into his thoughts" (Q. 22:52). Gabriel also gave Muhammad verses to replace the Satanic Verses. The reconciliation with the Meccan polytheists came to an end.

This story was widely rejected by the twelfth century. Some medieval scholars said that Satan imitated the Prophet's voice in pronouncing the Satanic Verses. Others dismissed the story entirely as a fabrication, which is the most common Muslim position today. The story was said to undermine the infallible transmission of the Qur'anic text and God's protection of the prophets from error. In addition, the chains of transmission did not meet the criteria for the authenticity of hadith reports. Three of the 30 versions of the story went back to the Successors of the Prophet, that is, the generation after the Prophet's Companions, but none could be traced back to Companions themselves.

Ibn Taymiyya, however, gives the Successor reports credence. When interpreting the Qur'an, he breaks with the philological method of other medieval Qur'an commentators. He does not normally interpret the Qur'an by examining the grammar and linguistic meaning of the text in the first instance. Instead, he interprets the Qur'an by following what the Qur'an says about itself and then what the Sunna, the Companions of the Prophet, and their Successors say it means. He locates the authoritative meaning of the Qur'an not in the findings of linguistic research but in what the earliest Muslims, the Salaf, said about the text. Additionally, Ibn Taymiyya accepts the authenticity of Successor reports concerning interpretation of the Qur'an and events in the life of the Prophet Muhammad, even if those reports are not sufficiently strong to establish matters of law. He maintains as well that there is no possibility of collusion or agreement on error when two or more chains transmitting a report go back to different Successors. The Satanic Verses story, with its three versions rooted in Successors, meets this criterion for authenticity, and Ibn Taymiyya has no difficulty accepting it.

Ibn Taymiyya also responds to theological objections to his view. One objection is that a sinning prophet does not provide a model of moral perfection. Ibn Taymiyya responds that there could be no repentance without sin. The Prophet provides the best model of repentance because he always repented from sin immediately. Sin with repentance is better than no sin at all, and repentance is a means of reaching perfection. This fits with Ibn Taymiyya's view of evil as divine pedagogy. Evil and sin serve to nurture greater religious awareness and worship of the one God. Ibn Taymiyya warns, however, that one should not sin intentionally merely to provide opportunity to repent. A second objection, common among Shi'is, is that people will find a sinning prophet repulsive. Ibn Taymiyya replies that no stigma attaches to sin from which one repents immediately. A third objection is that nothing guarantees that prophets will always repent. Ibn Taymiyya here invokes the distinctive truthfulness of prophets. God only chooses those of truthful character to be prophets. It was in fact the Satanic Verses incident that demonstrated the truthfulness of the Prophet Muhammad. When he fell into the snare of Satan, he sought the truth and did not try to hide his error or resist correction.

Posterity has not been kind to Ibn Taymiyya's doctrine of prophetic protection. Opponents through the centuries rejected his view as compromising the infallibility of the prophets. Even reformers and Salafis who take Ibn Taymiyya as their guiding light often obscure or ignore his teaching because it does not fit their own vision of Islamic orthodoxy.

THE SIGNS OF A TRUE PROPHET

The Satanic Verses episode raises the enduring Muslim theological question of how to discern a true prophet. For Ibn Taymiyya, the incident is part of what confirms Muhammad's truthfulness. It illustrates his ethical integrity and spiritual perfection. For early Ash'ari Kalam theologians, however, ethical considerations were irrelevant to verifying a prophet. Reason could not access ethical knowledge. God alone determined what was ethically right and wrong, and only divine revelation could provide this information. Human beings could not distinguish a true prophet from a false one on the basis of the prophet's character or ethical teaching. Only miracles could indicate the true prophet. A person who claimed to be a prophet and was confirmed by a miracle (*mu'jiza*) was truthful. The miracles of the Prophet Muhammad included the inimitable Qur'an and splitting the moon.

Most Mu'tazilis verified the truthfulness of the Prophet Muhammad through miracles as well. However, Mu'tazilis affirmed that reason knew the basics of right and wrong prior to revelation. Thus some Mu'tazilis did argue that prophets could be recognized as truthful by virtue of their superior moral character.

The later Ash'ari theologian al-Ghazali saw little difference between prophetic miracles on the one hand and magic and sorcery on the other. Miracles were unreliable as proofs of prophethood. So al-Ghazali located the proof of prophethood instead in the prophet's positive effects on the human soul, particularly as specified in the psychological writings of Avicenna.

Ibn Taymiyya agrees with al-Ghazali that miracles are not entirely adequate as proofs of prophethood, but he is not happy with al-Ghazali's solution. At the beginning of his large book *Prophetic Matters* (*Nubuwwat*), Ibn Taymiyya outlines three positions on miracles. First, for the Mu'tazilis a miracle is a matter of God breaking the custom of ordinary events (*kharq al-'ada*). God breaks custom only on behalf of prophets and never saints, magicians, or fortune-tellers. Thus a miracle necessarily indicates prophethood. Ibn Taymiyya is not averse to this view, as we shall see below.

Second, the early Ash'aris allow that custom-breaking miracles may occur at the hands of saints, magicians, and fortune tellers. However, say the Ash'aris, God will confirm only true claimants to prophethood with miracles, not false prophets. Ibn Taymiyya responds that this contradicts the Ash'aris' own principles. If God stands above all moral obligation, as the Ash'aris claim, then how can God be trusted to confirm only true prophets with miracles? There is nothing to prevent God from confirming a false prophet. Later in *Prophetic Matters*, Ibn Taymiyya insists that God would never confirm a false prophet because it would violate His wise purpose. He writes, "[God's] wise purpose necessitates that He make the truthfulness of the prophets obvious and support them" (*Nubuwwat* 906, trans. *Theodicy* 219).

Avicenna and philosophers of his type constitute the third position in Ibn Taymiyya's outline. Prophecy for Avicenna is an advanced intellectual power and the ability to transform rational knowledge into images in the imagination, as in visions and dreams. It is also the ability to make extraordinary things occur in the external world. This ability is the source of the miracles and wonders performed by prophets and others. Ibn Taymiyya criticizes Avicenna for reducing prophecy to a naturalistic phenomenon, as nothing more than a heightening of powers found in every human being, even in unbelievers. Ibn Taymiyya counters that in prophecy God imparts information to a prophet from outside himself. The Prophet Muhammad received his revelations from an angel that was separate from him. That angel was not merely an image in the Prophet's soul.

Ibn Taymiyya himself prefers to speak of "signs" (*ayat*) instead of "miracles" (*mu'jizat*) because the latter term is not used in the Qur'an, the Sunna of the Prophet, and the sayings of the Salaf. Similar to the Mu'tazilis, Ibn Taymiyya insists in *Prophetic Matters* that the signs of prophets are necessarily unique to them. They are not shared with sorcerers and magicians. However, not everything that breaks the custom of ordinary events counts as a prophetic sign. For Ibn Taymiyya custom is relative. Magic and fortune telling break the course of everyday events for most people, but they are customary for magicians and fortune tellers. Likewise, the customs of medical doctors, legal scholars, and astronomers are ordinary for those who practice those professions, but extraordinary for those who do not. Every profession and vocation has its unique and telltale signs that are well known throughout the human race. So in the same way and in the wise purpose of God, the signs of prophethood consist in customs that are specific to prophets.

According to Ibn Taymiyya, the signs customary to prophethood are transmission of truthful information from the world of the unseen and God's protection of that truth. Ibn Taymiyya acknowledges that fortune tellers and the jinn also provide information about the unseen, but he insists that they inevitably tell lies. They are intrinsically untrustworthy. Moreover, prophets bring information about the unseen that ordinary humans and jinn cannot access. For example, the signs that God showed the Prophet Muhammad on his Night Journey could not have been shown to the jinn.

Ibn Taymiyya's approach is circular, and he is well aware of it. He writes, "It is not known that a sign is specific to the prophet until prophecy is known" (*Nubuwwat* 174). To recognize a prophet requires first knowing what prophecy is. Ibn Taymiyya responds to this circularity by appealing to a long tradition of prophecy. He explains that God made Muhammad's prophethood obvious by linking him to earlier prophets. The Qur'an established the genus of prophecy by reciting the stories of previous prophets. These stories and the nature of prophecy were already known when the Prophet Muhammad appeared. Ibn Taymiyya writes, "[God] made plain that this genus of human beings [i.e. prophets] was known. Those equivalent to [Muhammad] and like him had preceded him, and so this was customary among human beings, even if it was infrequent among them" (*Nubuwwat* 187). Wide knowledge of the customs of prophets at the time Muhammad appeared left no excuse for not recognizing him as a prophet. Those who knew prophecy but rejected Muhammad were simply ignorant or stubborn.

In *Prophetic Matters*, Ibn Taymiyya pushes the problem of prophetic tradition back to its origin. How could humans recognize prophecy before God had established knowledge of prophecy among humankind? Ibn Taymiyya goes back to Noah, the first prophet after the great flood wiped out nearly the whole of humankind. He clarifies that God gave what was needed both to confirm the individual Noah as a prophet and to establish the species of prophecy more generally. Unfortunately Ibn Taymiyya does not explain how God established the species of prophecy at the time of Noah. Ultimately though, certainty of Muhammad's prophethood for Ibn Taymiyya is found in viewing the world through the lens of the Qur'an's prophetic narratives. The proof of prophethood is in recognizing its conformity to the prophetic pattern reprised in the Qur'an.

CHRISTIANITY: AN OBJECT LESSON IN INNOVATED RELIGION

However it was first established, Ibn Taymiyya maintains that the prophetic tradition confirmed and sealed by the Prophet Muhammad is revealed, rational, and definitive. In the year 1316 he received a direct challenge to this conviction in the form of the anonymous *Letter from the People of Cyprus* (*Risala min ahl jazirat Qubrus*). The *Letter* is a revision of an earlier Christian apologetic treatise. As Ibn Taymiyya himself notes, that earlier treatise had gained wide circulation. He replies to the *Letter* with his many times longer *Correct Answer* (*Al-Jawab al-sahih*).

Ibn Taymiyya's stated aim in *Correct Answer* is to set forth Christianity as an object lesson to Muslims about what innovation and heresy to avoid. He frequently draws parallels with errors he perceives among Sufis, Shi'is, and Kalam theologians. At the beginning of the tome, Ibn Taymiyya outlines the theological framework needed to position Christianity as a corruption of prophetic religion. The religion of all God's prophets and messengers is Islam, even if the various revelations such as the Torah, the Gospel, and the Qur'an differ in matters of religious practice. All other religion is polytheism and innovation. Furthermore, God singled out Muhammad as the best of the messengers and the Muslim community as the best of communities. The Muslim community provides the golden mean in matters of doctrine and practice that Jews and Christians take to extremes. The Jews and Christians have innovated the religions that they follow. They deviated from the revelations given to Moses and Christ, respectively. They failed to point to the definitive revelation given to Muhammad. Ibn Taymiyya explains further:

> The false religion of Christians is nothing but an innovated religion which they invented after the time of Christ and by which they changed the religion of Christ. Not only that, they strayed from the law (*shari'a*) of Christ to what they innovated. Then, when God sent Muhammad, they rejected him. Thus, their unbelief and error came to be of two aspects – that of changing the religion of the first messenger and of rejecting the second messenger. It is like the unbelief of the Jews who changed the legal prescriptions of the Torah before God's sending Christ, and then they rejected Christ. (*Jawab* 1:109–110, trans. *Response* 143)

The Christian *Letter* argues that Muhammad was only a prophet for the pagan Arabs by emphasizing that the revelation was only in Arabic. Ibn Taymiyya counters with Qur'anic texts like "We have only sent [Muhammad] to the entirety of humanity as a bringer of good news and as a warner" (Q. 34:28) to affirm that Muhammad's message is universal. Some Qur'anic verses may appear to limit the scope of his mission to the Arabs, but this does not undermine its universality.

Ibn Taymiyya adds that Muhammad was not mistaken or deluded into thinking that his message was universal. God would not permit that to happen to prophets.

The *Letter* continues that the Qur'an also praises Mary and Jesus and confirms the Christian scriptures in passages such as "We [i.e. God] have sent down to you the Book which declares true what came before it of the Torah and the Gospel" (Q. 3:3) and "If you are in doubt concerning what We have sent down to you, ask those who have been reading the Book before you" (Q. 10:94). The *Letter* concludes that the Qur'an is telling Christians to remain in their religion. Ibn Taymiyya agrees that the Qur'an confirms previous revelations. One must believe in all of God's books just as one must believe in all of God's prophets. However, he explains, the Qur'an does not confirm the innovated doctrines of the Christians.

As for the Bible itself, Ibn Taymiyya is careful, more so than some of his predecessors. Ibn Hazm (d. 1064) is well known for insisting that Jews and Christians had corrupted the very texts of their scriptures, and he compiled lists of contradictions and historical and theological errors to prove it. Unlike Ibn Hazm, Ibn Taymiyya says that textual corruption cannot be demonstrated or denied. While it is certain that Jews and Christians have corrupted the meaning of their texts, it cannot be known for sure whether the very texts have been altered. As a result, Ibn Taymiyya very rarely points out textual errors in the Bible. He instead interprets the texts to accord with his Islamic theological convictions, much as he seeks to fill the technical terminology of Sufism, Kalam theology, and philosophy with meanings corresponding to his understanding of the Qur'an and the Sunna.

This is readily apparent in *Correct Answer* in his discussion of the Christian doctrine of the Trinity. The *Letter* argues that the Trinity – the one God in three persons, Father, Son, and Holy Spirit – is proved by reason and supported by both the Bible and the Qur'an. Ibn Taymiyya discounts the *Letter*'s rational arguments, and he claims that the Trinity is a corruption of the religion of Christ inconsistent with the monotheism of the prophets. Neither the Bible nor the Qur'an supports the Christian doctrine. Ibn Taymiyya then reinterprets the Trinitarian names in the Gospel command to baptize "in the name of the Father, the Son, and the Holy Spirit" (Matt. 28:19) to fit his Qur'anic vision. "Father" means God; "Son" refers to the purely human prophet Christ; and "Holy Spirit" indicates either Gabriel, the angel of revelation, or the revelation itself. The text, according to Ibn Taymiyya, is telling readers to believe in God, God's prophet, and the angel who brought God's revelation.

The *Letter* makes two further key arguments. First, it explains that the Qur'an supports both the humanity and the divinity of Jesus. Ibn Taymiyya rejects the divinity of Jesus as incongruous with both reason and revelation. He reinterprets scriptural texts that might be misconstrued to imply that God dwelt in Christ. Second, the *Letter* claims that Islam is unnecessary because Christianity is the perfect religion. Judaism was the religion of law and justice while Christianity was the religion of grace. Ibn Taymiyya replies by placing Islam at the pinnacle of perfection instead of Christianity. Judaism focused on law and justice at the expense of grace. Christianity emphasized grace at the expense of justice and law. Islam perfectly balanced grace with law and justice. Ibn Taymiyya's vision of prophetic religion culminates in the Qur'an and the Prophet Muhammad. His *Correct Answer* sidelines Christianity as an irrational and unscriptural innovation, and his project of biblical interpretation seeks to rally the Jewish and Christian texts to the support of Islam.

THE ULTIMATE DESTINY OF UNBELIEVERS

Ibn Taymiyya is totally unsympathetic to religions apart from Islam, and he is in no doubt that unbelievers will suffer punishment in Hell-Fire in the hereafter. However, late in life he came to the conclusion that this punishment would not last forever. Sometime during Ibn Taymiyya's last imprisonment in Damascus, his student Ibn Qayyim al-Jawziyya asked him twice about the chastisement of unbelievers in Hell-Fire. The first time Ibn Taymiyya refused to answer. He would only say that it was a difficult question and it appears that he did not yet know what to think. The second time Ibn al-Qayyim sent his teacher a book containing a statement by 'Umar Ibn al-Khattab, a Companion of the Prophet Muhammad. The statement read, "Even if the People of the Fire stayed in the Fire like the amount of sand of 'Alij, they would have, despite that, a day in which they would come out." ('Alij was a large tract of sand on the way to Mecca.) Ibn Taymiyya responded with what appears to be his last work, a short treatise entitled *Refutation of Whoever Adheres to the Annihilation of Paradise and Hell-Fire* (*Al-Radd 'ala man qala bi-fana' al-janna wa al-nar*).

In this treatise, Ibn Taymiyya argues that it is incorrect to say that both Paradise and Hell-Fire will be annihilated. That was the view of an eccentric theologian from the second century of Islam. Instead, explains Ibn Taymiyya, the reward of Paradise is everlasting while the chastisement of unbelievers in Hell-Fire will end. 'Umar Ibn al-Khattab's statement elucidates the Qur'an, which says that those in Hell will be in it "for long stretches of time" (78:23). The expression "long stretches of time" does not mean forever. A time will come when everyone will come out.

Most other Muslim scholars of Ibn Taymiyya's day maintained that unbelievers would remain in Hell-Fire forever. The Qur'an says in many places that unbelievers will be in Hell-Fire "abiding therein forever" (e.g. Q. 4:169). It was also claimed that a consensus had been reached on this point. The Muslim scholars had come to agreement that unbelievers would remain in Hell-Fire forever with no end to their chastisement. There was also no disagreement among the earliest Muslim generations, the Salaf, over the matter.

Ibn Taymiyya responds that the Qur'anic terms "abiding" and "forever" should not be taken in their absolute senses. They do not preclude an eventual end to the punishment of unbelievers. He also rejects the alleged consensus around everlasting Hell-Fire. There was no consensus for this among the Companions, as the statement of the Companion 'Umar Ibn al-Khattab quoted above illustrates. Additionally, as mentioned in Chapter Five, Ibn Taymiyya does not accept a later consensus as binding because it is too difficult to verify.

Broader theological considerations also play a role in Ibn Taymiyya's argument. It follows from God's mercy and forgiveness that the blessings of Paradise will last forever, but everlasting chastisement does not follow from any of God's names and attributes. Also, God's mercy precludes chastisement without end. The Qur'an says, "[God] has written mercy for Himself" (Q. 6:12), and a hadith reads, "My mercy precedes my anger." Finally, Ibn Taymiyya appeals to God's wise purpose. God's wise purpose in chastisement is cleansing from sins and purifying souls, he explains. Therefore, there could be no wise purpose in chastising someone forever.

The implication of Ibn Taymiyya's argument is universal salvation. He makes clear that God's wise purpose in chastisement and punishment is reform and not retribution. Retribution metes out reward and punishment in due proportion to human deeds. The mainstream Sunni tradition maintained that the just retribution for unbelief was eternal Hell-Fire. From Ibn Taymiyya's perspective, however, everlasting punishment would defeat God's wise purpose of purifying souls toward a higher end. Hell-Fire fits neatly into Ibn Taymiyya's purpose-driven theology as an instrument of therapeutic discipline. Although Ibn Taymiyya does not say so explicitly, his reasoning leads to the conclusion that God will use Hell-Fire to bring all creatures into complete accord with the purposes for which they were naturally constituted and through which they will attain the greatest benefit. Everyone will eventually worship God alone.

For Ibn Taymiyya the ethic of both God and humanity is utilitarianism in the service of religion. Humans in an imperfect world should weigh up benefits and detriments in seeking what best promotes the religious law. Likewise, God creates and commands to maximize human benefit to the extent possible through correct worship. Ibn Taymiyya's God is a cosmic utilitarian who generates the greatest possible benefit for the greatest number. Simultaneously, this God elicits the worship, love, and praise that He alone is due. As we saw in Chapter Seven, God does not elicit human praise and love out of need. Nothing can add to God's immeasurably greater praise and love of Himself.

Ibn Taymiyya's thought overall gives priority to ethics and worship as obedience to God's law. That law includes speaking well of God and God's ways with humanity in order to render God due praise. Theology for Ibn Taymiyya is not a theoretical endeavor but a practical exercise directed toward obedience and worship. The whole of his intellectual project is a juristic enterprise devoted to delineating and rationalizing the correct way to worship God.

9

EPILOGUE

The jihadi group al-Qaeda is well known for carrying out the September 11, 2001 attacks on the World Trade Center in New York City and the Pentagon in Washington DC. Earlier, in August 1996, al-Qaeda issued a declaration of jihad against Americans. In this statement, al-Qaeda's leader Osama Bin Laden complained that American soldiers were stationed in Saudi Arabia. After Iraq invaded Kuwait in 1990, the Americans had placed large numbers of troops in Saudi Arabia to protect the oil fields and to drive Iraq out of Kuwait. Bin Laden blamed the American presence for causing Saudi Arabia's economic woes and for compromising the Islamic integrity of the country. Saudi Arabia's rulers were effectively supporting unbelievers against Muslims. To address these problems, Bin Laden called on Muslims to join together to attack the Americans and drive them out of Arabia. Muslims must put aside their differences to accomplish this task. Even those not practicing their religion must help. One must choose the lesser of two harms. The harm in using imperfect Muslims to fight would be less than the harm caused by unbelievers occupying Muslim lands.

Bin Laden supported his analysis by quoting nearly a full page from the shortest of Ibn Taymiyya's three famous anti-Mongol fatwas (MF 28:501–508). As noted in Chapter One, Ibn Taymiyya argues in this fatwa that the harm or detriment in fighting the Mongols is less than the detriment in not fighting them. One must choose the lesser of two harms, and in this case fighting the invaders was the lesser harm. Moreover, even immoral Muslims must be rallied to contribute to jihad. God supports His religion with those who are bad sinners when it is a matter of bad sinners defending Islam against those who are even more sinful. The military leaders and most of the soldiers in jihad might be bad sinners, but that is better than falling to an invader who would cause even greater harm to religion and human prosperity. Bin Laden reasoned likewise. Jihadis do not need to be pious. They simply need to be willing to fight for the greater good of the religion as al-Qaeda understood it.

Not long after al-Qaeda's pronouncement, the Egyptian jihadi group al-Gama'a al-Islamiyya used Ibn Taymiyya's utilitarian reasoning to a different end. The Gama'a had launched terror attacks against the Egyptian government and tourist industry from the late 1980s into the 1990s. They had declared the Egyptian government apostate for not fully upholding Islamic law and had taken up arms to impose an Islamic state by force. Then, in 1997, Gama'a leaders began calling for an end to the violence. In 2002 they issued a number of manifestos revoking their jihad against the Egyptian state. One of these manifestos was *The Initiative to Stop the Violence* (*Mubadarat waqf al-'unf*).

The Gama'a's *Initiative* appealed to several medieval sources to make its argument. One of these was a short treatise by Ibn Taymiyya on weighing up benefits and detriments (MF 20:48–61). Ibn Taymiyya's treatise begins, "The Law came to obtain benefits and perfect them, to obstruct detriments and reduce them. It makes preponderate the best of what is good and the least of what is evil. [It came] to obtain the greatest of two benefits by foregoing the lesser of the two and to repel the greater of two detriments by bearing the lesser of the two" (MF 20:48). Ibn Taymiyya goes on to explain his utilitarian principles along lines similar to those in his anti-Mongol fatwa quoted by Bin Laden. A lesser evil may be used to repel a greater evil. Likewise, it is permitted to use a lesser evil to obtain a greater benefit, and it is permitted to forgo a lesser good in order to obtain a greater good.

On this basis, the Gama'a al-Islamiyya reasoned that Islamic law forbade their earlier violence because of its extremely harmful and detrimental effects. Their violence killed a lot of people and led to the destruction of homes and mosques. The political grievances remained, but the violence had not brought any benefit. Therefore the proper way forward was patience in the face of oppression. Patience would be worth more on the Day of Judgement than the wanton violence of earlier years. Moreover, their terrorism and bloodshed had given Islam a bad name in the outside world. Islam's enemies, especially the Americans and the Israelis, had exploited that bad name to their own advantage.

The Gama'a also explained that they should have known better than to have launched their violent jihad in the first place. They should have seen that there was no justification for declaring the Egyptian government apostate. They should have understood that Islam obligated calculating the benefits and detriments of actions ahead of time. They had failed by focusing too much on the details of scriptural texts and had lost sight of the larger objectives of the religion. In 2004 the Gama'a criticized al-Qaeda in similar fashion. They accused al-Qaeda of making jihad an end in itself instead of a means to the end of promoting religion. Al-Qaeda had forgotten the priority of preaching and persuasion and made violent jihad primary instead. Like the Gama'a itself earlier on, al-Qaeda focused too narrowly on texts promoting violence and ignored the overall aims of Islam.

Comparing al-Qaeda and the Gama'a's use of Ibn Taymiyya is instructive. Like Ibn Taymiyya, both groups sought to advance their vision of Islam above all else. Both faced the problem of an imperfect world in which Islam was perceived to be under existential threat. Both turned to Ibn Taymiyya's utilitarian reasoning to discern the way forward and, with their different assessments of political reality, they came to opposite conclusions. Ibn Taymiyya's religious utilitarianism does not always lead to the same ends.

Ibn Taymiyya's broader legacy has also been complex. He did not have much impact on mainstream religion in the Mamluk Empire. Nevertheless, his works were read and debated in Damascus and Cairo well into the fifteenth century. Among his disciples, Ibn Qayyim al-Jawziyya embraced Ibn Taymiyya's outlook most vigorously and comprehensively. Ibn al-Qayyim was prolific, and his elaborate and systematic style made Taymiyyan ideas accessible to a wider audience. As a result, the Shafi'i chief judge of Damascus, Taqi al-Din al-Subki, confronted and intimidated Ibn al-Qayyim in the 1340s over God's attributes, the duration of Hell-Fire, and other matters. The writings of al-Subki and other fourteenth and fifteenth-century opponents of Ibn Taymiyya established polemical fault lines on intercession, divorce, and theology that reverberate down to the present.

Reception of Ibn Taymiyya's ideas has often been selective. For example, the Yemeni scholar Ibn al-Wazir (d. 1436) drew on Ibn Taymiyya and Ibn Qayyim al-Jawziyya to formulate a theology mediating between Sunnism and Zaydi Shi'ism. Ibn al-Wazir adopted Ibn Taymiyya's theology of wise purpose in God's will while leaving aside the question of temporally originating events in God's essence. He also allowed that Ibn Taymiyya's arguments for limited chastisement of unbelievers in Hell-Fire constituted an acceptable Islamic position. Ibn al-Wazir himself, however, preferred to withhold judgement on the issue.

The Qadizadeli reform movement in the seventeenth-century Ottoman Empire provides another example of selective use of Ibn Taymiyya. The two key intellectuals informing the Qadizadelis were Birgili Mehmed Efendi (d. 1573) and Ahmad al-Aqhisari (d. 1631 or 1634). Both were Hanafis who followed the Maturidi school of Kalam theology that originated in central Asia. Like the later Ash'ari theologians, the Maturidis denied that God had a body, and they reinterpreted non-literally God's attributes that implied corporeality. Despite their lack of affinity with Taymiyyan theology, Birgili and al-Aqhisari both drew on Ibn Taymiyya and Ibn al-Qayyim to warn against the dangers of visiting graves. Al-Aqhisari also borrowed and paraphrased from Ibn Taymiyya's *The Necessity of the Straight Path* (*Iqtida' al-sirat al-mustaqim*) to work out his own views on religious innovation.

In the modern period, Ibn Taymiyya's writings on theology and innovated practices have inspired reform movements of diverse kinds. These include the puritan Wahhabis in Arabia from the eighteenth century onward, Salafi reform initiatives in south Asia and the Arab world beginning in the nineteenth century, and the contemporary Global Salafism movement that originated in Saudi Arabia in the 1960s. Salafis are among the most avid readers of Ibn Taymiyya today. They adopt Ibn Taymiyya's theological framework over against Ash'arism, but they are not always comfortable with his views on more controversial questions like the duration of Hell-Fire and the Prophet's protection from sin and error.

In addition to the Salafis, modernists and revivalists have drawn on Ibn Taymiyya to present visions of Islam open to the contemporary world. The Pakistani modernist Fazlur Rahman (d. 1988) writes approvingly of Ibn Taymiyya's reinjection of divine wise purpose into mainstream Islamic thought, and he commends his ethical reformulation of Sufism for modern Muslim reform. The Qatari-based revivalist Yusuf al-Qaradawi (b. 1926) invokes Ibn Taymiyya's utilitarianism and political pragmatism to encourage Muslims to engage constructively in democratic and pluralist societies. Muslims should seek justice and the common good to the best of their abilities, even in a society ruled by unbelievers.

To conclude, Ibn Taymiyya was both fecund and polarizing in his own lifetime, and he remains so today. His life and writings continue to inspire Muslims seeking a distinctively ethical vision of Islam grounded in the Qur'an and the Sunna of the Prophet. His criticisms of Ash'arism, Ibn al-'Arabi, Shi'ism, Christianity, and shrine religion still stoke tensions within the Muslim community and beyond. Whether as boon or as bane, Ibn Taymiyya is playing a key role in the ongoing negotiation of what Islam means.

BIBLIOGRAPHY

Sources quoted in the text are listed below by their abbreviations. MF is the largest modern collection of Ibn Taymiyya's writings. Ibn Taymiyya's books named in the text but not quoted are not listed; the same applies to works by other medieval scholars. For an introduction to modern editions of Ibn Taymiyya's Arabic corpus, see https://sites.google.com/site/jhoover363/taymiyyan-studies/arabic-texts

Bidaya = Ibn Kathir. *Al-Bidaya wa al-nihaya*. Ed. 'Abd al-Qadir Arna'ut and Bashshar 'Awwad Ma'ruf. 20 vols. 2nd printing. Damascus: Dar Ibn Kathir, 2010.

Dar' = Ibn Taymiyya. *Dar' ta'arud al-'aql wa al-naql*. Ed. Muhammad Rashad Salim. 11 vols. Riyadh: Jami'at al-Imam Muhammad Ibn Su'ud al-Islamiyya, 1411/1991.

Durra = Al-Subki, Taqi al-Din. *Al-Durra al-mudiyya fi al-radd 'ala Ibn Taymiyya*. Damascus: Matba'at al-taraqi, 1929.

FK = Ibn Taymiyya. *Al-Fatawa al-kubra*. Ed. Muhammad 'Abd al-Qadir 'Ata and Mustafa 'Abd al-Qadir 'Ata. 6 vols. Beirut: Dar al-kutub al-'ilmiyya, 1987.

Jawab = Ibn Taymiyya, *Al-Jawab al-sahih li-man baddala din al-Masih*. Ed. 'Ali Ibn Hasan Ibn Nasir, 'Abd al-'Aziz Ibn Ibrahim al-'Askar, and Hamdan Ibn Muhammad al-Hamdan. 7 vols. 2nd ed. Riyadh: Dar al-'asima, 1999.

JR = *Jami' al-rasa'il li-Ibn Taymiyya*. Ed. Muhammad Rashad Salim. Vol. 1. Cairo: Matba'at al-madani, 1969.

Kanz = Ibn al-Dawadari, Abu Bakr Ibn 'Abd Allah. *Kanz al-durar wa jami' al-ghurar*. Vol. 9, *Al-Durar al-fakhir fi sirat al-Malik al-Nasir*. Ed. Hans Robert Roemer. Cairo: Qism al-dirasat al-islamiyya bi-l-ma'had al-almani li-l-athar bi-l-Qahira, 1960.

Mahabba = Ibn Taymiyya. *Qa'ida fi al-mahabba*. Ed. Muhammad Rashad Salim. Cairo: Maktabat al-turath al-islami, n.d.

Masalik = Al-ʻUmari, Ahmad Ibn Yahya Ibn Fadl Allah. "Masalik al-absar fi mamalik al-amsar." In *Al-Jamiʻ li-sira Shaykh al-Islam Ibn Taymiyya*, ed. Muhammad ʻUzayr Shams and ʻAli Ibn Muhammad al-ʻUmran, 312–28. 2nd printing. Mecca: Dar ʻalam al-fawa'id, 1422/2001–2.

MF = *Majmuʻ fatawa Shaykh al-Islam Ahmad Ibn Taymiyya*. Ed. ʻAbd al-Rahman Ibn Muhammad Ibn Qasim and Muhammad Ibn ʻAbd al-Rahman Ibn Muhammad. 37 vols. Riyadh: Matabiʻ al-Riyad, 1961–67.

Minhaj = Ibn Taymiyya. *Minhaj al-sunna al-nabawiyya fi naqd kalam al-Shiʻa al-Qadariyya*. Ed. Muhammad Rashad Salim. 9 vols. Riyadh: Jamiʻat al-Imam Muhammad Ibn Suʻud al-Islamiyya, 1406/1986.

Muhassal = Al-Razi, Fakhr al-Din. *Al-Muhassal*. Ed. Taha ʻAbd al-Ra'uf Saʻd. Cairo: Maktabat al-kulliyyat al-azhariyya, n.d.

Nubdha = Al-Dhahabi, Shams al-Din. "Nubdha min sirat Shaykh al-Islam Ibn Taymiyya." In "A New Source for the Biography of Ibn Taymiyya." Ed. and trans. Caterina Bori. *Bulletin of the School of Oriental and African Studies* 67.3 (2004): 321–48.

Nubuwwat = Ibn Taymiyya, *Kitab al-nubuwwat*. Ed. ʻAbd al-ʻAziz Ibn Salih al-Tuwayyan. 2 vols. Riyadh: Adwa' al-salaf, 2000.

Public Duties = Ibn Taymiya. *Public Duties in Islam: The Institution of the Hisba*. Trans. Muhtar Holland. Leicester: The Islamic Foundation, 1985.

Response = Michel, Thomas F. *A Muslim Theologian's Response to Christianity: Ibn Taymiyya's Al-Jawab Al-Sahih*. Delmar, NY: Caravan, 1984.

Siyasa = Ibn Taymiyya. *Al-Siyasa al-sharʻiyya fi islah al-raʻi wa al-raʻiyya*. Ed. ʻAli Ibn Muhammad al-ʻUmran. Mecca: Dar al-fawa'id, 1429/2008.

Theodicy = Hoover, Jon. *Ibn Taymiyya's Theodicy of Perpetual Optimism*. Leiden: Brill, 2007.

ʻUqud = Ibn ʻAbd al-Hadi, Muhammad Ibn Ahmad. *Al-ʻUqud al-durriyya min manaqib Shaykh al-Islam Ahmad Ibn Taymiyya*. Ed. Muhammad Hamid al-Fiqi. Cairo: Matbaʻat al-hijazi, 1938.

Following are the main European language sources consulted in the writing of this book. For fuller bibliographies of scholarship on Ibn Taymiyya, his context, and his legacy, see https://sites.google.com/site/jhoover363/taymiyyan-studies

Ahmed, Shahab. "Ibn Taymiyyah and the Satanic Verses." *Studia Islamica* 87 (1998): 67–124.

Aigle, Denise. "The Mongol Invasions of Bilad Al-Sham by Ghazan Khan and Ibn Taymiyah's Three 'Anti-Mongol' Fatwas." *Mamluk Studies Review* 11.2 (2007): 89–120.

Al-Gama'ah al-Islamiyah. *Initiative to Stop the Violence (Mubadarat waqf al-'unf): Sadat's Assassins and the Renunciation of Political Violence*. Trans. Sherman A. Jackson. New Haven, CT: Yale University Press, 2015.

Ali, Mohamed M. Yunis. *Medieval Islamic Pragmatics: Sunni Theorists' Models of Textual Communication*. Richmond, Surrey: Curzon, 2000.

Al-Jamil, Tariq. "Ibn Taymiyya and Ibn al-Mutahhar al-Hilli: Shi'i Polemics and the Struggle for Religious Authority in Medieval Islam." In *Ibn Taymiyya and His Times*, ed. Yossef Rapoport and Shahab Ahmed, 229–46. Karachi: Oxford University Press, 2010.

Al-Matroudi, Abdul Hakim I. *The Hanbali School of Law and Ibn Taymiyyah: Conflict or Conciliation*. London: Routledge, 2006.

______. "The Removal of Blame from the Great *Imams:* An Annotated Translation of Ibn Taymiyyah's *Raf' al-Malam 'an al-A'immat al-A'lam*." *Islamic Studies* 46.3 (2007): 317–80.

Amitai, Reuven. "The Mongol Occupation of Damascus in 1300: A Study of Mamluk Loyalties." In *The Mamluks in Egyptian and Syria Politics and Society*, ed. Michael Winter and Amalia Levanoni, 21–39. Leiden: Brill, 2004.

Anjum, Ovamir. *Politics, Law, and Community in Islamic Thought: The Taymiyyan Moment*. Cambridge, UK: Cambridge University Press, 2012.

Antrim, Zayde. "The Politics of Place in the Works of Ibn Taymiyah and Ibn Fadl Allah al-'Umari." *Mamluk Studies Review* 18 (2014–15): 91–111.

Assef, Qais. "Le soufisme et les soufis selon Ibn Taymiyya." *Bulletin d'études orientales* 60 (2011): 91–121.

Belhaj, Abdessamad. "Law and Order According to Ibn Taymiyya and Ibn Qayyim al-Jawziyya: A Re-Examination of *siyasa shar'iyya*." In *Islamic Theology, Philosophy and Law: Debating Ibn Taymiyya and Ibn Qayyim Al-Jawziyya*, ed. Birgit Krawietz and Georges Tamer, 400–421. Berlin: de Gruyter, 2013.

Bell, Joseph Norment. *Love Theory in Later Hanbalite Islam*. Albany, NY: State University of New York Press, 1979.

Bori, Caterina. *Ibn Taymiyya: una vita esemplare. Analisi delle fonti classiche della sua biografia*. Supplemento N. 1. *Rivista Degli Studi Orientali*. Vol. 76. Pisa/Roma: Istituti Editoriali e Poligrafici Internazionali, 2003.

______. "The Collection and Edition of Ibn Taymiyah's Works: Concerns of a Disciple." *Mamluk Studies Review* 13.2 (2009): 47–67.

______. "Ibn Taymiyya *wa-Jama'atu-hu*: Authority, Conflict and Consensus in Ibn Taymiyya's Circle." In *Ibn Taymiyya and His Times*, ed. Yossef Rapoport and Shahab Ahmed, 23–52. Karachi: Oxford University Press, 2010.

______. "Theology, Politics, Society: The Missing Link. Studying Religion in the Mamluk Period." In *Ubi Sumus? Quo Vademus? Mamluk Studies – State of the Art*, ed. Stephan Conermann, 57–94. Göttingen: V&R unipress, Bonn University Press, 2013.

______. "One or Two Versions of *al-Siyasa al-Shar'iyya* of Ibn Taymiyya? And What Do They Tell Us?" ASK Working Paper 26. Bonn: Annemarie Schimmel Kolleg, 2016.

______. "Ibn Taymiyya (14th to 17th Century): Transregional Spaces of Reading and Reception." *The Muslim World* 108.1 (2018): 87–123.

Bori, Caterina and Livnat Holtzman, eds. *A Scholar in the Shadow: Essays in the Legal and Theological Thought of Ibn Qayyim Al-Ǧawziyyah*. *Oriente Moderno* monograph series 90.1, 2010.

Broadbridge, Anne F. *Kingship and Ideology in the Islamic and Mongol Worlds*. Cambridge, UK: Cambridge University Press, 2008.

Chamberlain, Michael. *Knowledge and Social Practice in Medieval Damascus, 1190–1350*. Cambridge: Cambridge University Press, 1994.

Cook, Michael. *Commanding Right and Forbidding Wrong in Islamic Thought*. Cambridge, UK: Cambridge University Press, 2000.

el Omari, Racha. "Ibn Taymiyya's 'Theology of the Sunna' and his Polemics with the Ash'arites." In *Ibn Taymiyya and His Times*, ed. Yossef Rapoport and Shahab Ahmed, 101–119. Karachi: Oxford University Press, 2010.

El-Rouayheb, Khaled. "From Ibn Hajar al-Haytami (d. 1566) to Khayr al-Din al-Alusi (d. 1899): Changing Views of Ibn Taymiyya among non-Hanbali Sunni Scholars." In *Ibn Taymiyya and His Times*, ed. Yossef Rapoport and Shahab Ahmed, 269–318. Karachi: Oxford University Press, 2010.

______. "Theology and Logic." In *The Oxford Handbook of Islamic Theology*, ed. Sabine Schmidtke, 408–31. Oxford: Oxford University Press, 2016.

El-Tobgui, Carl Sharif. "From Legal Theory to *Erkenntnistheorie*: Ibn Taymiyya on *Tawatur* as the Ultimate Guarantor of Human Cognition." *Oriens* 46.1–2 (2018): 6–61.

Farrukh, Omar A., trans. *Ibn Taimiyya on Public and Private Law in Islam*. Beirut: Khayat, 1966.

Fons, Emmanuel. "À propos des Mongols, une lettre d'Ibn Taymiyya au Sultan al-Malik al-Nasir Muhammad b. Qalawun." *Annales Islamologiques* 43 (2009): 31–73.

Friedman, Yaron. *The Nusayri-'Alawis: An Introduction to the Religion, History, and Identity of the Leading Minority in Syria*. Leiden: Brill, 2010.

Griffel, Frank. "Al-Ġazali's Concept of Prophecy: The Introduction of Avicennan Psychology into Aš'arite Theology." *Arabic Sciences and Philosophy* 14 (2004): 101–44.

______. "Ibn Taymiyya and His Ash'arite Opponents on Reason and Revelation: Similarities, Differences, and a Vicious Circle." *The Muslim World* 108.1 (2018): 11–39.

Hallaq, Wael B. *Ibn Taymiyya against the Greek Logicians*. Oxford, UK: Clarendon Press, 1993.

Hassan, Mona. "Modern Interpretations and Misinterpretations of a Medieval Scholar: Apprehending the Political Thought of Ibn Taymiyya." In *Ibn Taymiyya and His Times*, ed. Yossef Rapoport and Shahab Ahmed, 338–66. Karachi: Oxford University Press, 2010.

______. *Longing for the Lost Caliphate: A Transregional History*. Princeton, NJ: Princeton University Press, 2016.

Heck, Paul L. "Jihad Revisited." *Journal of Religious Ethics* 32 (2004): 95–128.

Hofer, Nathan. *The Popularisation of Sufism in Ayyubid and Mamluk ouk Egypt, 1173–1325*. Edinburgh: Edinburgh University Press, 2015.

Holtzman, Livnat. "The Dhimmi's Question on Predetermination and the Ulama's Six Responses: The Dynamics of Composing Polemical Didactic Poems in Mamluk Cairo and Damascus." *Mamluk Studies Review* 16 (2012): 1–54.

______. *Anthropomorphism in Islam: The Challenge of Traditionalism (700-1350)*. Edinburgh: Edinburgh University Press, 2018.

______. "The Bedouin Who Asked Questions: The Later Hanbalites and the Revival of the Myth of Abu Razin al-'Uqali." In *Islamic Philosophy from the 12th to the 14th Century*, ed. Abdelkader Al Ghouz, 431–68. Göttingen: V&R unipress, Bonn University Press, 2018.

Homerin, Th. E. "Ibn Taimiya's *Al-Sufiyya wa-al-fuqara'*." *Arabica* 32 (1985): 219–44.

Hoover, Jon. "Perpetual Creativity in the Perfection of God: Ibn Taymiyya's Hadith Commentary on God's Creation of this World." *Journal of Islamic Studies* 15.3 (2004): 287–329.

______. *Ibn Taymiyya's Theodicy of Perpetual Optimism*. Leiden: Brill, 2007.

______. "Islamic Universalism: Ibn Qayyim al-Jawziyya's Salafi Deliberations on the Duration of Hell-Fire." *The Muslim World* 99.1 (2009): 181–201.

______. "God Acts by His Will and Power: Ibn Taymiyya's Theology of a Personal God in his Treatise on the Voluntary Attributes." In *Ibn Taymiyya and His Times*, ed. Yossef Rapoport and Shahab Ahmed, 55–77. Karachi: Oxford University Press, 2010.

______. "Ibn Taymiyya." In *Christian-Muslim Relations: A Bibliographical History*, Vol. 4 *(1200–1350)*, ed. David Thomas and Alex Mallett, 824–78. Leiden: Brill, 2012.

______. "A Muslim Conflict over Universal Salvation." In *Alternative Salvations: Engaging the Sacred and the Secular*, ed. Hannah Bacon, Wendy Dossett, and Steve Knowles, 160–71. London: Bloomsbury, 2015.

______. "Ibn Taymiyya between Moderation and Radicalism." In *Reclaiming Islamic Tradition: Modern Interpretations of the Classical Heritage*, ed. Elisabeth Kendall and Ahmad Khan, 177–203. Edinburgh: Edinburgh University Press, 2016.

_____. "Withholding Judgment on Islamic Universalism: Ibn al-Wazir (d. 840/1436) on the Duration and Purpose of Hell-Fire." In *Locating Hell in Islamic Traditions*, ed. Christian Lange, 208–37. Leiden: Brill, 2016.

_____. "Ibn Taymiyya's Use of Ibn Rushd to Refute the Incorporealism of Fakhr al-Din al-Razi." In *Islamic Philosophy from the 12th to the 14th Century*, ed. Abdelkader Al Ghouz, 469–91. Göttingen: V&R unipress, Bonn University Press, 2018.

_____. "Foundations of Ibn Taymiyya's Religious Utilitarianism." In *Philosophy and Jurisprudence in the Islamic World*, ed. Peter Adamson, 145–168. Berlin: De Gruyter, 2019.

_____. "Early Mamluk Ash'aris against Ibn Taymiyya on the nonliteral reinterpretation of God's attributes (*ta'wil*)." In *Philosophical Theology in Islam: The Later Ash'arite Tradition*, ed. Jan Thiele and Ayman Shihadeh. Leiden: Brill, forthcoming.

Hoover, Jon with Marwan Abu Ghazaleh Mahajneh. "Theology as Translation: Ibn Taymiyya's Fatwa Permitting Theology and Its Reception into His *Averting the Conflict between Reason and Revealed Tradition* (Dar' Ta'arud al-'Aql wa l-Naql)." *The Muslim World* 108.1 (2018): 40–86.

Ibn Taymiyya. *Public Duties in Islam: The Institution of the Hisba*. Trans. Muhtar Holland. Leicester: The Islamic Foundation, 1985.

Ibn Taymiyya. *Epistle on Worship* (Risalat al-'Ubudiyya). Trans. James Pavlin. Cambridge: Islamic Texts Society, 2015.

Irwin, Robert. *The Middle East in the Middle Ages: The Early Mamluk Sultanate 1250–1382*. London: Croom Helm, 1986.

Jackson, Sherman A. "Ibn Taymiyyah on Trial in Damascus." *Journal of Semitic Studies* 39.1 (1994): 41–85.

Johansen, Baber. "A Perfect Law in an Imperfect Society: Ibn Taymiyya's Concept of 'Governance in the Name of the Sacred Law'." In *The Law Applied: Contextualizing the Islamic Shari'a. A Volume in Honor of Frank E. Vogel*, ed. Peri Bearman, Wolfhart Heinrichs and Bernard G. Weiss, 259–93. London: I. B. Tauris, 2008.

Jokisch, Benjamin. "*Ijtihad* in Ibn Taymiyya's *fatawa*." In *Islamic Law: Theory and Practice*, ed. R. Gleave and E. Kermeli, 119–37. London: I. B. Tauris, 1997.

Karamustafa, Ahmet T. *God's Unruly Friends: Dervish Groups in the Islamic Later Middle Period 1200–1550*. Salt Lake City, UT: University of Utah Press, 1994.

Khalil, Mohammad Hassan. *Islam and the Fate of Others: The Salvation Question*. Oxford: Oxford University Press, 2012.

Knysh, Alexander D. *Ibn 'Arabi in the Later Islamic Tradition: The Making of a Polemical Image in Medieval Islam*. Albany, NY: State University of New York Press, 1999.

Krawietz, Birgit and Georges Tamer, eds. *Islamic Theology, Philosophy and Law: Debating Ibn Taymiyya and Ibn Qayyim Al-Jawziyya*. Berlin: de Gruyter, 2013.

Laoust, Henri. *Essai sur les doctrines sociales et politiques de Taḳi-d-Din Ahmad b. Taimiya, canoniste hanbalite né à Harran en 661/1262, mort à Damas en 728/1328*. Cairo: Imprimerie de l'institut français d'archéologie orientale, 1939.

_____. "La Biographie d'Ibn Taimiya d'après Ibn Katir." *Bulletin d'études Orientales* 9 (1942–43): 115–62.

_____. *La profession de foi d'Ibn Taymiyya:* La Wasitiyya. Paris: Librairie orientaliste Paul Geuthner, 1986.

Little, Donald P. "The Historical and Historiographical Significance of the Detention of Ibn Taymiyya." *International Journal of Middle East Studies* 4 (1973): 311–27.

_____. "Did Ibn Taymiyya Have a Screw Loose?" *Studia Islamica* 41 (1975): 93–111.

Makdisi, George. "Ibn Taimiya: A Sufi of the Qadiriya Order." *American Journal of Arabic Studies* 1 (1973): 118–29.

Mazor, Amir. *The Rise and Fall of a Muslim Regiment: The Mansuriyya in the First Mamluk Sultanate, 678/1279–741/1341*. Göttingen: V&R unipress, Bonn University Press, 2015.

Meijer, Roel, ed. *Global Salafism: Islam's New Religious Movement*. London: Hurst & Company, 2009.

Memon, Muhammad Umar. *Ibn Taimiya's Struggle against Popular Religion: With an Annotated Translation of His* Kitab iqtida' as-sirat al-mustaqim mukhalafat ashab al-jahim. The Hague: Mouton, 1976.

Michel, Thomas F. *A Muslim Theologian's Response to Christianity: Ibn Taymiyya's* Al-Jawab Al-Sahih. Delmar, NY: Caravan, 1984.

Michot, Yahya M. [Jean R. Michot, Yahya J. Michot] *Musique et danse selon Ibn Taymiyya: Le livre du samâ' et de la danse* (Kitâb al-samâ' wa l-raqs) *compilé par le Shaykh Muhammad al-Manbiji*. Paris: J. Vrin, 1991.

_____. *Ibn Taymiyya: Lettre a un roi croisé (Al-Risâlat al-qubrusiyya)*. Louvain-la-Neuve: Bruylant-Academia, 1995.

_____. "Vanités intellectuelles...l'impasse des rationalismes selon le *Rejet de la contradiction* d'Ibn Taymiyyah." *Oriente Moderno* 19 (2000): 597–617.

_____. "Un célibataire endurci et sa maman: Ibn Taymiyya (m. 728/1328) et les femmes." *Acta Orientalia Belgica* 15 (2001): 165–90.

_____. "A Mamluk Theologian's Commentary on Avicenna's *Risala Adhawiyya*: Being a Translation of a Part of the *Dar' al-ta'arud* of Ibn Taymiyya, with Introduction, Annotation, and Appendices." *Journal of Islamic Studies* 14.2 (2003): 149–203 (Part I), 14.3 (2003): 309–63 (Part II).

_____. *Ibn Taymiyya: Muslims under Non-Muslim Rule*. Oxford: Interface Publications, 2006.

_____. "Between Entertainment and Religion: Ibn Taymiyya's Views on Superstition." *The Muslim World* 99.1 (2009), 1–20.

______. "Ibn Taymiyya's 'New Mardin Fatwa'. Is Genetically Modified Islam (GMI) Carcinogenic?" *Muslim World* 101.2 (2011): 130–81.

______. *Ibn Taymiyya: Against Extremisms*. Beirut: Albouraq, 2012.

______. "An Important Reader of al-Ghazali: Ibn Taymiyya." *The Muslim World* 103.1 (2013): 131–60.

______. "Ibn Taymiyya, Salafism and Mercy." In *Tarihte ve Günümüzde Selefilik*, ed. Ahmet Kavas, 411–30. Istanbul: Ensar Neşriyat, 2014.

______. "Ibn Taymiyya's Critique of Shi'i Imamology." *The Muslim World* 104.1–2 (2014): 109–49.

______. "Al-Ghazalis Esotericism According to Ibn Taymiyya's *Bughyat al-Murtad*." In *Islam and Rationality: The Impact of al-Ghazali. Papers Collected on His 900th Anniversary*. Vol. 1, ed. Georges Tamer, 345–74. Leiden: Brill, 2015.

______. "Ibn Taymiyya's Commentary on Avicenna's *Isharat, namat* X." In *Islamic Philosophy from the 12th to the 14th Century*, ed. Abdelkader Al Ghouz, 119–210. Göttingen: V&R unipress, Bonn University Press, 2018.

Mirza, Younus Y. "Ishmael as Abraham's Sacrifice: Ibn Taymiyya and Ibn Kathir on the Intended Victim." *Islam and Christian–Muslim Relations* 24.3 (2013): 277–98.

______. "Ibn Taymiyya as Exegete: Moses' Father-in-Law and the Messengers in Surat Ya Sin." *Journal of Qur'anic Studies* 19.1 (2017): 39–71.

Morel, Teymour. "Deux textes anti-Mongols d'Ibn Taymiyya." *The Muslim World* 105.3 (2015): 368–97.

Murad, Hasan Qasim. "Ibn Taymiya on Trial: A Narrative Account of His Mihan." *Islamic Studies* 18 (1979): 1–32.

Mustafa, Abdul Rahman. "Ibn Taymiyyah & Wittgenstein on Language." *The Muslim World* 108.3 (2018): 465–91.

Olesen, Niels Henrik. *Cultes des saints et pélerinages chez Ibn Taymiyya*. Paris: Paul Geuthner, 1991.

Opwis, Felicitas. *Maslaha and the Purpose of the Law: Islamic Discourse on Legal Change from the 4th/10th to 8th/14th Century*. Leiden: Brill, 2010.

Özervarli, M. Sait. "The Qur'anic Rational Theology of Ibn Taymiyya and His Criticism of the Mutakallimun." In *Ibn Taymiyya and His Times*, ed. Yossef Rapoport and Shahab Ahmed, 78–100. Karachi: Oxford University Press, 2010.

______. "Divine Wisdom, Human Agency and the *fitra* in Ibn Taymiyya's Thought." In *Islamic Theology, Philosophy and Law: Debating Ibn Taymiyya and Ibn Qayyim Al-Jawziyya*, ed. Birgit Krawietz and Georges Tamer, 37–60. Berlin: de Gruyter, 2013.

Post, Arjan. "A Glimpse of Sufism from the Circle of Ibn Taymiyya: An Edition and Translation of Al-Ba'labakki's (d. 734/1333) Epistle on the Spiritual Way (*Risalat Al-Suluk*)." *Journal of Sufi Studies* 5.2 (2016): 156–87.

Rapoport, Yossef. "Legal Diversity in the Age of *Taqlid*: The Four Chief *Qadis* under the Mamluks." *Islamic Law and Society* 10.2 (2003): 210–28.

_____. *Marriage, Money and Divorce in Medieval Islamic Society*. Cambridge: Cambridge University Press, 2005.

_____. "Ibn Taymiyya's Radical Legal Thought: Rationalism, Pluralism and the Primacy of Intention." In *Ibn Taymiyya and His Times*, ed. Yossef Rapoport and Shahab Ahmed, 191–226. Karachi: Oxford University Press, 2010.

_____. "Royal Justice and Religious Law: *Siyasah* and Shari'ah under the Mamluks." *Mamluk Studies Review* 16 (2012): 71–102.

Rapoport, Yossef, and Shahab Ahmed, eds. *Ibn Taymiyya and His Times*. Karachi: Oxford University Press, 2010.

Sarrió Cucarella, Diego. "Corresponding across religious borders: the letter of Ibn Taymiyya to a Crusader in Cyprus." *Islamochristiana* 36 (2010): 187–212.

_____. "Spiritual Anti-Elitism: Ibn Taymiyya's Doctrine of Sainthood (*walaya*)." *Islam and Christian–Muslim Relations* 22.3 (2011): 275–91.

Schallenbergh, Gino. "Ibn Taymiya (d. 1328) on Chess: Legal Evidence for a Prohibition." In *Egypt and Syria in the Fatimid, Ayyubid and Mamluk Eras V*, ed. Urbain Vermeulen and Kristof D'Hulster, 525–37. Leuven: Peeters, 2007.

Sheikh, Mustapha. *Ottoman Puritanism and Its Discontents: Ahmad al-Rumi al-Aqhisari and the Qadizadelis*. Oxford: Oxford University Press, 2016.

Shoshan, Boaz. *Popular Culture in Medieval Cairo*. Cambridge, UK: Cambridge University Press, 1993.

Suleiman, Farid. *Ibn Taymiyya und die Attribute Gottes*. Berlin: de Gruyter, 2019.

Talhamy, Yvette. "The Fatwas and the Nusayri/Alawis of Syria." *Middle Eastern Studies* 46.2 (2010): 175–94.

Taylor, Christopher S. *In the Vicinity of the Righteous: Ziyara and the Veneration of Muslim Saints in Late Medieval Egypt*. Leiden: Brill, 1999.

Ukeles, Raquel M. "The Sensitive Puritan? Revisiting Ibn Taymiyya's Approach to Law and Spirituality in Light of 20th-century Debates on the Prophet's Birthday (*mawlid al-nabi*)." In *Ibn Taymiyya and His Times*, ed. Yossef Rapoport and Shahab Ahmed, 319–37. Karachi: Oxford University Press, 2010.

Vasalou, Sophia. *Ibn Taymiyya's Theological Ethics*. New York: Oxford University Press, 2016.

Von Kügelgen, Anke. "Dialogpartner im Widerspruch: Ibn Rushd und Ibn Taymiya über die 'Einheit der Wahrheit'." In *Words, Texts and Concepts Cruising the Mediterranean Sea: Studies on the Sources, Contents and Influences of Islamic Civilization and Arabic Philosophy and Science Dedicated to Gerhard Endress on His Sixty-Fifth Birthday*, ed. R. Arnzen and J. Thielmann, 455–81. Leuven: Peeters, 2004.

_____. "The Poison of Philosophy: Ibn Taymiyya's Struggle for and against Reason." In *Islamic Theology, Philosophy and Law: Debating Ibn Taymiyya and Ibn Qayyim Al-Jawziyya*, ed. Birgit Krawietz and Georges Tamer, 253–328. Berlin: de Gruyter, 2013.

Winter, Stefan. *A History of the 'Alawis: From Medieval Aleppo to the Turkish Republic*. Princeton, NJ: Princeton University Press, 2016.

Zouggar, Nadjet. "L'impeccabilité du prophète Muhammad dans le credo sunnite d'al-As'ari (m. 324/935) à Ibn Taymiyya (m. 728/1328)." *Bulletin d'études orientales* (Damascus) 60 (2011): 73–90.

_____. "Aspects de l'argumentation élaborée par Taqi l-Din Ahmad b. Taymiyya (m. 728/1328) dans son *Livre du rejet de la contradiction entre raison et Écriture (Dar' ta'arud al-'aql wa-l-naql)*." *Arabica* 61.1–2 (2014): 1–17.

INDEX

Terms beginning with the Arabic definite article al- are alphabetized by what follows the hyphen.